THE
GREAT
AMERICAN
TRIVIA BOOK

★ IN FACTS WE TRUST ★

DANIEL ADAMS

Adamsmedia
Avon, Massachusetts

Published by
Adams Media, a division of F+W Media, Inc.
57 Littlefield Street, Avon, MA 02322. U.S.A.
www.adamsmedia.com

Contains material adapted and abridged from *The Everything® American History Book, 2nd Edition* by John R. McGeehan, MA, copyright © 2007 by F+W Media, Inc., ISBN 10: 1-59869-261-5, ISBN 13: 978-1-59869-261-7; *The Everything® Kids' Presidents Book* by Brian Thornton, copyright © 2007 by F+W Media, Inc., ISBN 10: 1-59869-262-3, ISBN 13: 978-1-59869-262-4; *The Everything® Kids' States Book* by Brian Thornton, copyright © 2007 by F+W Media, Inc., ISBN 10: 1-59869-263-1, ISBN 13: 978-1-59869-263-1.

ISBN 10: 1-4405-7360-3
ISBN 13: 978-1-4405-7360-6
eISBN 10: 1-4405-7361-1
eISBN 13: 978-1-4405-7361-3

Printed in the United States of America.

10 9 8 7 6 5 4 3 2 1

Library of Congress Cataloging-in-Publication Data

Adams, Daniel.
    The great American trivia book / Daniel Adams.
       pages cm
    Includes index.
    ISBN 978-1-4405-7360-6 (pb) -- ISBN 1-4405-7360-3 (pb) -- ISBN 978-1-4405-7361-3 (ebook) -- ISBN 1-4405-7361-1 (ebook)
    1. United States--History--Miscellanea. I. Title.
    E179.A19 2014
    973--dc23
                              2013035927

Cover image © Juniperimages Corporation and 123rf.com.
Images © 123rf.com.

This book is available at quantity discounts for bulk purchases.
For information, please call 1-800-289-0963.

★ CONTENTS ★

INTRODUCTION

DID YOU KNOW that Philadelphia was our nation's first capital or that more men perished in prisons than in any battle during the Civil War? How about that a real estate investigation is what led to the discovery of Bill Clinton's widely publicized affair?

No matter how much you know about American history, you'll find that there's always another fun fact to learn, and now *The Great American Trivia Book* gives you hundreds of quick tidbits of trivia to add to your repertoire. Whether you want to refresh your memory or just want a retelling that won't cause you to nod off, this book takes you on an exciting journey through the nation's most important moments. From Christopher Columbus's theft of a crewmember's reward to Richard Nixon's Saturday Night Massacre to George W. Bush's $40 million inauguration celebration, you'll not only learn about what Americans have done throughout the years, but also the unbelievable facts surrounding these historical accounts. Filled with fascinating details and stories, this book gives you a glimpse into the events and legacies that have impacted our history from the birth of our nation to recent history.

So forget the dry details about presidents, declarations, and laws that you'll find in other books, and dive into an unforgettable exploration of America's past. With the indispensable facts in *The Great American Trivia Book*, you're guaranteed to view the nation's wild history in a whole new light!

CHAPTER 1

A WHOLE NEW WORLD AND EARLY AMERICA

By the time Christopher Columbus sailed across the Atlantic Ocean, the civilizations on the American continents were already centuries old, so it makes less sense to say that Columbus discovered a new world than to say that he uncovered a very old one. But as you'll find out from the following tidbits about American history, he was not even the first European to set foot in the Americas or the one to establish colonies in the New World. French explorers led some of these expeditions, and the English some others. In fact, some of their explorations occurred almost concurrently. This chapter will discuss what really happened during Columbus's voyage and how those early explorers and settlers survived living in the New World in its first fledgling years.

IN HIS TEENS, Christopher Columbus sailed commercial routes between Genoa and other Mediterranean ports before voyages to the Aegean island of Chios (near what is now Turkey), England, the Portuguese island of Madeira, and Guinea (on Africa's west coast).

IT'S OFTEN BELIEVED that Columbus had to work hard to convince the king and queen, as well as his crew, that Earth was spherical rather than flat. However, at the end of the fifteenth century, the idea of a round world was not a new concept. Even some ancient Greeks like Aristotle were aware of Earth's roundness.

THE SEAFARER WAS commissioned with the promise that he would receive one-tenth of the profits from the expeditions, and he was granted titles, including "Admiral of the Ocean Sea," viceroy, and governor of whatever lands he discovered.

FERDINAND AND ISABELLA had promised that the first man to sight land would get a yearly pension of 10,000 maravedis (Spanish gold coins). A few hours after midnight on October 12, 1492, Juan Rodriguez Bermeo, a lookout on the *Pinta*, spotted what was most likely an island of the Bahamas, but Columbus claimed to have spied land first and collected the reward himself.

COLUMBUS BELIEVED HE had found Asia when he landed in the Bahamas, but actually he'd miscalculated the distance, and a few other minor details. In fact, to say he misjudged would be an understatement. Some believe he underestimated Earth's size by 25 percent. Many people, including Columbus, thought the oceans were far smaller than they really are and that the land masses were much larger. His crew wasn't the least bit pleased that their journey took as long as it did. There were rumblings of mutiny.

THESE EUROPEAN SETTLERS discovered not only a new land, but new ways of living and eating as well. For instance, the Arawak (in the Bahamas) and Taino (in the Caribbean) slept in hand-woven hamacas, or hammocks. Columbus's men discovered a new diet of corn (maize), sweet potatoes, and red chili pepper, and they learned to grow squash, pumpkins, and beans. Then there was the botanical novelty the inhabitants smoked—tobacco.

NOT LONG BEFORE this time, a decree called the Treaty of Toledo, signed in 1479, had divided Portuguese and Spanish territories. This gave Portugal territorial rights to Morocco and other areas, and prohibited Spain from sailing beyond the Canary Islands. It is thought that Columbus may have intentionally reported the latitude of his discoveries incorrectly, knowing full well that these islands belonged to Portugal by the terms of the treaty.

THE TRIP IN 1502 was the fastest Columbus ever sailed. He organized the entire fleet in roughly four weeks, with the goal of circumnavigating the world. He left on May 9, 1502, only three months after the new "Governor of the Indies" had been sent off, but he was forbidden to return to Hispaniola.

SIR WALTER RALEIGH was an English adventurer, writer, explorer, and, for a while, the favorite of Queen Elizabeth I. In 1584, he established the first settlement on Roanoke Island, off of what is known today as North Carolina.

———————— ★ ————————

SIR WALTER RALEIGH'S new colony was not only the first Roanoke settlement, but also the first English colony in America.

———————— ★ ————————

IN 1605, TWO groups of London merchants who had combined the investments of many smaller investors petitioned King James I for a charter to establish another colony in Virginia. These two groups—prototypes of modern-day corporations—became the Virginia Company of London and the Plymouth Company.

———————— ★ ————————

THE VIRGINIA COMPANY promised to provide free passage to America in exchange for a contract under which the settlers agreed to seven years of indentured servitude. This became a popular arrangement, and in December 1606, a total of 120 people agreed to these terms and boarded three vessels—the *Susan Constant*, the *Discovery*, and the *Godspeed*.

———————— ★ ————————

BY MAY 1607, the 104 remaining settlers sailed the three rather frail vessels through the Chesapeake Bay and thirty miles up the James River to reach a parcel of densely wooded, swampy land. There, the settlers built Jamestown, England's first permanent colony.

———————— ★ ————————

THE JAMESTOWN COLONISTS arrived too late in the season to plant crops, and the swamps didn't help their chances of survival. Many of these people were not able to adapt to the harsh conditions and within a few months, died of famine and disease, while others went to live with Native American tribes. Only thirty-eight made it through their first year in the New World.

EVERYONE KNOWS ABOUT Jamestown in Virginia and about Plymouth in Massachusetts, but St. Augustine in Florida is actually the oldest city in North America. Spanish settlers established it in 1565, almost fifty years before Jamestown!

MOST PEOPLE KNOW Captain John Smith from the tales of Pocahontas, but he was a crusader and pirate before he became the gentleman everyone knows.

SMITH WAS CHOSEN to lead the Jamestown Colony in 1608, but he became a bit of a dictator, ruling with harsh orders such as "no work, no food." He turned the settlers into foragers and successful traders with the Native Americans, who taught the English how to plant corn and other crops.

SMITH LED EXPEDITIONS to explore the regions surrounding Jamestown, and it was during one of these that the chief of the Powhatan Native Americans captured Smith. According to an account Smith published in 1624, he was going to be put to death until the chief's daughter, Pocahontas, saved him. Evidence is scarce that Pocahontas actually helped John Smith, risking her life to save him. An account that is probably more accurate states that Smith participated in an initiation ceremony making him an honorary Powhatan tribesman.

———————— ★ ————————

POCAHONTAS'S REAL NAME was Matoaka. The Native American name "Pocahontas" means "playful one."

———————— ★ ————————

THE JAMESTOWN SETTLERS did capture a young Pocahontas around 1612, returning her to their colony. In captivity, she caught the eye of John Rolfe, an Englishman, who later married her with the blessing of her father and the English governor. This established a peace with the Powhatans that lasted eight years.

———————— ★ ————————

WHEN ROLFE AND Pocahontas moved to England, she converted to Christianity and took the name Rebecca.

———————— ★ ————————

IN THEIR VERY first years in Virginia, the British encouraged interracial marriage with the Native Americans in order to promote better relations. In Virginia, money was offered to white Virginians who would marry Native Americans. However, few took advantage of the offer.

———————— ★ ————————

EVENTUALLY, THE ENGLISH forbid interracial marriage. Pocahontas was one of the last Native Americans to be accepted into British-American society through marriage.

———————— ★ ————————

THE TOBACCO PLANT in the Americas can be traced back more than 8,000 years. Native Americans eventually started smoking and chewing the dried tobacco leaves, and by the time Europeans came to North America, tobacco was growing in abundance in the Americas.

SETTLERS PLANTED TOBACCO crops in every available inch of fertile soil, but once indentured servitude ended, they were hard-pressed to maintain their tobacco and other crops. They began purchasing laborers from Dutch traders who kidnapped black Africans from their homelands, transported them against their will across the ocean, and sold them to plantation owners— the start of slavery in America.

RELATIONS WITH THE Native Americans began to sour, for the natives frequently attacked Jamestown. In 1622, 350 colonists were killed. By 1644, a total of 500 had perished.

IN 1676, THE Jamestown colonists rebelled against the rule of Governor William Berkeley in what's known as Bacon's Rebellion. A group of former indentured servants, led by plantation owner Nathaniel Bacon, didn't think Berkeley was protecting them from Native American raids. When Bacon and his men formed a small army to punish the Native Americans, Berkeley denounced them as rebels. Marching against Jamestown in 1676, Bacon captured the town and burned it.

HIRED BY THE Dutch to find the Northwest Passage to Asia, English explorer Henry Hudson sailed into the wonderfully sheltered bay at Manhattan Island, one of the greatest natural harbors in the world, in September 1609. Spurred by Hudson's tales of a fur-trading paradise, the Dutch West India Company colonized this new region in 1624, calling it New Netherlands. The following year, they established a Dutch trading post, named New Amsterdam, on Manhattan's southern tip.

———————— ★ ————————

AFTER SETTLING IN Manhattan, the Dutch began other settlements in the Bronx, Brooklyn, Queens, and Staten Island, building a fortification to protect the colony from potential English or Native American invasions. This wall encompassed the area we now know as Wall Street.

———————— ★ ————————

ANOTHER SETTLEMENT THEY created was Coney Island. Many historians believe that the name was chosen because the Dutch word for rabbit was "konijn" and the barrier beach island had a large population of wild rabbits.

———————— ★ ————————

WHEN THE BRITISH invaded New Amsterdam in 1664, Peter Stuyvesant, then the governor, vowed to fight them, but later relented in order to not ruin the city. The new English governor offered free passage back to Holland for those who didn't wish to stay, but reportedly no one left. Two days later, the settlement was renamed New York.

———————— ★ ————————

AS A BIRTHDAY present to his brother, King Charles named the settlement of New York after the Duke of York on August 29, 1664.

NOT EVERY PILGRIM wanted religious freedom. The Pilgrims recruited a number of others to join them on their voyage. Approximately eighty "strangers," who weren't Separatists or Puritans, decided to sail as well for better lives, adventure, shipboard jobs, and, of course, great wealth.

THE *MAYFLOWER* WASN'T the only ship meant to carry the Pilgrims over to the Virginia Colony—the group had obtained a charter to set sail on two ships, the *Speedwell* and the *Mayflower*. Twice during the summer months they set sail, and twice they returned to England on account of the *Speedwell*, because it wasn't exactly a seaworthy vessel. So the *Mayflower* headed out alone, sailing from Plymouth, England, in September 1620.

THE *MAYFLOWER* SPENT two months crossing an angry Atlantic Ocean, and to make matters worse, the maps the Pilgrims used weren't all that trustworthy. Those maps, along with the strong winds, took the sailors well north of the Virginia Colony. On November 21, 1620, the Pilgrims reached Provincetown Harbor at the point of Cape Cod, Massachusetts.

BECAUSE THERE WAS dissension among the *Mayflower*'s passengers, they drew up an agreement while anchored in the harbor. The Mayflower Compact was the first colonial agreement that formed a government by the consent of those governed, for the signers agreed to follow all "just and equal" laws that the settlers enacted. Furthermore, the majority would rule in matters where there was disagreement. That might seem simple today, but back then, this was a giant leap away from the tradition of royal and absolute rulers.

WHEN THE PILGRIMS established Plymouth Colony, they chose this site for its farm fields, its supply of fresh drinking water, and the hill that enabled them to build a fort. But by early 1621, the Pilgrims were cold, hungry, and sick. They had arrived too late to plant crops, and with the snow, cold, and dwindling food supply, as many as half the colonists died.

★

A NATIVE AMERICAN named Samoset, who entered their settlement speaking English, saved the Pilgrims. Samoset said he'd heard them speaking and learned their language, and evidently he saw their needs. He brought along Squanto to help teach the Pilgrims how to survive with new methods of farming and fishing, and soon the Pilgrims learned to plant corn and fertilize their fields.

★

SQUANTO ACTED AS the interpreter between the Pilgrims and the great Chief Massasoit of the Wampanoag in southeastern Massachusetts. The two sides pledged not to harm one another, and by the following autumn in 1621, the Pilgrims celebrated their first harvest with their Native American neighbors.

★

THE FIRST THANKSGIVING lasted three days, and both the Pilgrims and Wampanoag tribe brought provisions for the feast.

★

NATIVE AMERICANS HAD celebrated autumn harvests for centuries. Early New Englanders celebrated Thanksgiving only when there was a plentiful harvest, but it gradually became an annual custom. During the American Revolution, the Continental Congress proposed a national day of thanksgiving, and in 1863, Abraham Lincoln issued the proclamation designating the fourth Thursday in November as Thanksgiving Day.

BETWEEN 1629 AND 1640, more than 20,000 additional colonists made the crossing to settle in New England.

LED BY JOHN Endecott, Massachusetts Bay Colony's government was first established in England, and later moved to Massachusetts in 1629.

WHILE PEOPLE USE the term "puritanical" to describe rigid morality or narrowness of mind nowadays, Puritanism's values of hard work, a good business sense, and the need for education were the traits that represented what America was all about during this time.

THE PURITANS PROVED to be as intolerant as the king they had fled. Attendance at Sunday services was mandatory, and with the work required to thrive in the colonies, that left little leisure time. The punishment for any crime committed was harsh, and those who spoke out against the puritanical dictates were persecuted.

THE QUAKERS WERE banished from the Massachusetts Bay Colony when they dared to disagree, and others fled for religious and economic reasons. Among them was Roger Williams, a Puritan minister, who founded a settlement around 1635 that became the colony of Rhode Island.

———————— ★ ————————

IN 1674, ENGLAND tried to subdue the rebellious Massachusetts Bay colonists, charging that they had violated the Navigation Acts, among other misdeeds. In 1684, England revoked the Massachusetts Bay Colony's charter, and in 1691, the colony was granted a new royal charter that essentially ended the form of government the Puritans had created. The right to elect representatives was now based on property qualifications rather than church membership.

———————— ★ ————————

IN PURITAN TIMES, the term "witch" was applied to a poor, old person who was also contentious.

———————— ★ ————————

THE SALEM WITCH Trials were started by two girls: nine-year-old Betty Parris and her eleven-year-old cousin Abigail Williams. In 1692, they began acting quite strangely, running around the house, flapping their arms, screaming, and throwing themselves around the room. The local doctors were at a loss to explain their antics, so they blamed witchcraft. Betty and Abigail identified the Parris family's West Indian slave, Tituba, as their tormentor, before adding other names such as Sarah Good and Sarah Osborne.

———————— ★ ————————

SO-CALLED WITCHES REPORTEDLY had identifiable marks on their bodies—marks put there by the Devil himself—that professional witch finders could identify, since the witches were insensitive to pain. The witch finders had monetary incentive to identify new subjects, as they were paid a fee for every witch conviction.

NINETEEN PEOPLE WERE executed in the wake of the Salem Witch Trials, until public opinion turned against the accusers and local judges. In 1696, the General Court adopted a resolution of repentance. Although the Puritan influence declined, the Congregational churches remained dominant in Massachusetts into the nineteenth century.

EVEN WITH A royal governor, colonists got an early taste of independence. The Puritans' belief that communities were formed by covenants led to the creation of town meetings, the first democratic institution in America. At town meetings, every church member could speak, those who were male and held property could vote, and the decision of the majority ruled. In some towns, men who were not property holders could also vote. This democratic atmosphere later led to fewer restrictions regarding religious and personal freedoms.

IN THE NEW England Puritan town, no one was more important than its minister. Ministers were expected to be well educated. Thus, Puritans laid the foundations of education in the colonies, with America's first secondary school established in 1635.

HARVARD COLLEGE (now Harvard University) began in 1636 as an institution to train ministers.

———————— ★ ————————

THE PEQUOT WAR of 1637 was the first major war fought in New England. Connecticut declared war on the Pequot tribe, and the colonists launched a surprise attack that included setting a Pequot village on fire. Few Pequot survived in the aftermath. Some may have been sold into slavery, while others fled throughout New England.

———————— ★ ————————

KING PHILIP'S WAR between Anglos and the Wampanoag, Narragansett, and Nipmuck in the mid-1670s resulted in enormous casualties for both sides. Approximately one-sixteenth of the white male population of New England died in the fighting, and the total casualties, Anglo and Native, exceeded those of the French and Indian War, the Revolution, the War of 1812, the Mexican War, and the Spanish-American War combined.

———————— ★ ————————

KING WILLIAM'S WAR broke out in 1689 after England's William III entered the War of the League of Augsburg against France. Native Americans, provoked by the French to attack, ravaged the English settlements in New England and New York. Retaliating, New Englanders gained control of Port Royal, a key French post in Nova Scotia.

———————— ★ ————————

KING WILLIAM'S WAR lasted for at least six years until the Treaty of Ryswick in 1697 halted both sides, restoring Port Royal to the French. However, this war accomplished nothing, for the treaty merely declared that the prewar positions would remain. As a result, the unresolved tensions led to further fighting.

QUEEN ANNE'S WAR broke out in 1702. English colonists captured and burned Saint Augustine, Florida (then Spanish territory). There were massacres at the hands of French troops and their Native American allies in the colonies, and troops also tried again to wrest away control of Port Royal. The British and colonists conquered Acadia in 1710, but failed to encroach on Quebec and Montreal.

WHEN THE TREATY of Utrecht ended Queen Anne's War in 1713, it ceded Acadia, as well as Newfoundland and the Hudson Bay territory, to the British. Cape Breton Island stayed French.

SAMUEL DE CHAMPLAIN produced the first accurate chart of the Atlantic coast, from Newfoundland to Cape Cod, as well as maps of the Saint Lawrence Valley and the Great Lakes. Champlain also created a trading post in what is now Quebec City, and established the commercial and military alliances that endured to the end of the French regime in Canada.

KING GEORGE'S WAR broke out in 1744. The French captured and destroyed a British fort at Canso, Nova Scotia, and they took prisoners to their fortress at Cape Breton Island. Fearing the French, the governor of Massachusetts enlisted further colonial aid. Thus a militia of 4,000 sailed in British ships and fought under the command of Sir William Pepperell, a Maine merchant. King George's War ended in 1748 with the Treaty of Aix-la-Chapelle.

THE FRENCH AND Indian War finally decided the question of colonial control. It broke out in 1754 and lasted until 1763. It officially started when Virginia's governor tried unsuccessfully to warn the French to get out of British territory by dispatching an armed force under the command of George Washington to drive off the French. But the French had a surprise for Washington, and they defeated his troops at the Battle of Fort Necessity in 1754, sending Washington back to Virginia.

THE TREATY OF Paris in 1763 ended more than a century and a half of French power in the New World. French control of Canada went to Britain, and France ceded all of its territories east of the Mississippi River to the British as well. Spain also gave Florida to the British.

IN WINNING THE French and Indian War, Britain doubled its national debt and took on more territory than it could easily manage. The British tried to compel colonists to pay for these campaigns against French Canada, but this did not sit well with the American colonies.

PARLIAMENT LEVIED HIGH duties on various commodities needed in the colonies—everyday items, such as molasses and sugar. Thus, the Sugar Act, passed in 1764, became the first significant tax demanded of colonists.

———————— ★ ————————

THE CURRENCY ACT prevented the colonies from issuing their own money. All transactions had to be made with gold. This angered the independent-minded colonists, who did not want to be financially dependent on England.

———————— ★ ————————

THE ACTS OF Trade and Navigation, commonly known as Navigation Acts, were designed to protect commerce. It stated that the colonists could ship particular items, such as tobacco, rice, and indigo, only to another British colony or to the mother country. That meant the colonists were not permitted to trade with other countries. The Navigation Acts weren't repealed until 1849.

———————— ★ ————————

THE QUARTERING ACT of 1765 declared that colonial citizens would have to provide food and housing for royal troops, a decree that understandably cast a financial hardship on the colonists and was a blatant invasion of their personal privacy.

———————— ★ ————————

THE STAMP ACT required colonists to pay extra for newspapers, land deeds, dice, and card games—even graduation diplomas, since every paper document would require a revenue stamp from a British agent.

———————— ★ ————————

THE COLONISTS, WHO earnestly held to the belief that these taxes were the result of their lack of representation in the British Parliament, were infuriated by the Stamp Act. Interestingly enough, Prime Minister Grenville had given the colonies an opportunity to avert Parliament's stamp tax and create a tax of their own to meet the costs of maintaining troops in the colonies. The colonists did not take advantage of this opportunity.

PRIOR TO THE enactment of the Grenville Program in 1765, the Crown's taxes on the colonists had been external—in other words, taxes on commerce that America engaged in with the rest of the world (i.e., tariffs). The Stamp Act, passed on March 22, 1765, was the first internal tax, a tax on activities of the colonists within their own localities.

THE TOWNSHEND ACTS levied tariffs on imports such as glass, lead, paint, and tea. The colonial protest was alive and well, and in April 1770, Parliament repealed the Townshend taxes, except for the levy on tea.

THE SONS OF Liberty, which featured leaders such as Samuel Adams, John Hancock, and Paul Revere, was created to oppose the Stamp Act. This secret, patriotic society kept meeting after the Act was repealed in 1766, forming the Committees of Correspondence that fostered resistance to British economic control.

JOHN HANCOCK WAS a Harvard-educated patriot who became a colonial businessman, and a rather wealthy one, after inheriting his mercantile firm. Elected to the Massachusetts legislature, Hancock was soon at odds with the British government in 1768, when customs officials seized his sloop after he failed to pay import duties on his cargo. His zealous defense won him popularity among the factions of people opposed to British control of the colonies.

PAUL REVERE, a silversmith and engraver, was also a patriot. His elegant silverware, bowls, pitchers, and tea sets were favorites of Boston aristocracy, but he also used his talents to make artificial teeth, surgical instruments, and engraved printing plates.

SAMUEL ADAMS WAS a law student and merchant who was educated at Harvard. But when his own ventures failed, he joined his father in a brewery business. He was also active in Boston political circles and was elected to the lower house of the General Court before being promoted to the Boston chapter of the Sons of Liberty.

THE BOSTON MASSACRE occurred on March 5, 1770, when a group of colonists living in Boston were demonstrating in front of the not-too-popular Customs House, where British troops had been called to quell the American protests. The squad of soldiers responded by firing shots into the crowd, killing five protestors.

CRISPUS ATTUCKS, the leader of the group of protesting colonists at the Boston Massacre, became the first to die for American liberty. Attucks was of mixed descent, most likely a man of black, white, and Native American heritage. In 1888, a monument was erected in the Boston Common to honor Attucks and the others who gave their lives for liberty.

PAUL REVERE'S ENGRAVING of the Boston Massacre is a good example of colonial propaganda. Revere shows the British soldiers standing in a straight line and firing point-blank into a mostly unarmed, defenseless group of colonists. Most eyewitness accounts did not agree with Revere's depiction of the event.

WHEN HALF A million pounds of tea was sent to the four primary ports—Philadelphia, New York, Charleston, and Boston—anti-British sentiment rallied to the point that tea-laden ships turned back from Philadelphia and New York, unable to unload. The governor was adamant that colonists pay the levy, so in December 1773, as the loaded ships sat at anchor, Samuel Adams, Paul Revere, and some fifty patriots (some dressed as Native Americans) boarded the ships and dumped 343 chests of tea into Boston Harbor. This bold act, known as the Boston Tea Party, incurred the king's wrath; in response, he closed the port of Boston and imposed a military form of government.

_____ ★ _____

IN SEPTEMBER AND October of 1774, colonial leaders met in Philadelphia's Carpenters' Hall for the First Continental Congress. The Massachusetts House of Representatives had called for an intercolonial congress that would take any actions necessary to preserve or establish colonial rights. Only Georgia was not represented among the fifty-five delegates of the First Continental Congress.

———————— ★ ————————

PHILADELPHIA WAS THE first capital of the United States. For a number of years both during and after the American Revolution, Philadelphia was our national capital. The capital moved to New York during President Washington's administration.

———————— ★ ————————

IF SOMEONE REBELLED against the British Crown, he would be dragged to the gallows, hanged by the neck, and then cut down alive; his entrails would be taken out and burned while he was still alive; his head would be cut off and his body divided into four parts.

———————— ★ ————————

STILL HOPING TO reconcile their complaints with the British Crown, the delegates approved the Declaration of Rights and Grievances. Members of this First Continental Congress concluded their sessions by agreeing to meet again, in May 1775, to vote on stronger measures if the British had not addressed their grievances. They had taken the first steps toward freedom.

———————— ★ ————————

IN JANUARY 1776, political philosopher Thomas Paine wrote a fifty-page pamphlet titled "Common Sense." The pamphlet went through twenty-five editions in 1776 and sold hundreds of thousands of copies. Although it was published anonymously, it rallied the masses. In fact, General Washington ordered that Paine's pamphlets be read to his troops to inspire them to fight even harder for freedom.

———————— ★ ————————

BRITISH ORDERS HAD been sent to General Thomas Gage, then governor of Massachusetts, advising him to arrest dissidents and to capture their arms and munitions. On April 19, Gage ordered British troops to Concord, where he'd learned of a stockpiled arsenal. On the evening of April 18, Paul Revere, William Dawes, and Samuel Prescott rode ahead to warn John Hancock and Samuel Adams, two patriots whom Gage wanted to arrest. Revere's historic midnight ride has become part of American folklore.

MANY RECOUNTS OF Revere's ride, like Henry Wadsworth Longfellow's ballad "Paul Revere's Ride," are slightly exaggerated. In fact, the British detained Revere while he was en route with his message.

THE WARNING OF the British's arrival sent by Paul Revere, William Dawes, and Samuel Prescott urged fifty minutemen to meet the British advance guard in Lexington. When the British major John Pitcairn ordered the patriots to disperse, a pistol shot rang out. Who fired this first shot is not entirely clear, but one thing was certain: British troops opened fire on the minutemen even as the colonists retreated. By the time the firing stopped, eight minutemen were killed and ten wounded.

BY THE TIME the redcoats reached Boston, at least 270 British soldiers were dead, missing, or wounded in battle—a higher number than the colonial casualties.

THE TERM "MINUTEMAN" is used to describe an armed man who could be prepared "in a minute's notice" to fight against the British during the Revolutionary War.

———————— ★ ————————

ON MAY 10, 1775, the Second Continental Congress convened in Philadelphia to determine the fate of the colonies' relationship with Britain. It took the delegates some time to gather, but by June, sixty-five delegates had arrived, representing twelve colonies (Georgia wasn't represented until September). Richard Henry Lee, representing Virginia, moved that the colonies absolve themselves of allegiance to the British Crown. John Adams of Massachusetts seconded the motion, but action was deferred until July.

———————— ★ ————————

IN THE NIGHT hours of June 16, 1775, colonial militia took up positions on Breed's Hill, adjacent to Bunker Hill overlooking Boston Harbor. General Gage, eager to avenge his losses at Concord, was determined to take the hill. The next day, 3,000 redcoats marched up Breed's Hill in close ranks, and it wasn't until they marched close enough (approximately forty paces from colonial forces) that American troops opened fire, causing the British to suffer severe casualties and forcing them to retreat.

———————— ★ ————————

EVEN THOUGH THE battle occurred at Breed's Hill, it's been misnamed the Battle of Bunker Hill and is known as one of the bloodiest encounters in the Americans' struggle for freedom.

———————— ★ ————————

AFTER THE BATTLE of Bunker Hill, the Second Continental Congress commissioned Virginia's George Washington to take command of the American forces. Washington's Continental army, a small, dependable regiment, arrived in Cambridge on July 3, 1775, where the new commander in chief took over. Washington refused any payment for his services, except for expenses.

THE BATTLE OF Bunker Hill left too much bloodshed to permit peace or compromise. The Second Continental Congress requested that Benjamin Franklin, Thomas Jefferson, John Adams, Roger Sherman, and Robert R. Livingston draft a formal protest against Britain, in line with Lee's resolution, declaring the colonies free of British rule. The resulting document was the Declaration of Independence, which not only outlined the grievances against Britain and declared the colonies free and independent, but also incorporated John Locke's doctrine of unalienable rights, including life and liberty.

THE DECLARATION OF Independence went through eighty-four revisions, and on July 4, 1776, Congress adopted the declaration by unanimous vote of the delegates of twelve colonies. Only New York abstained, because representatives had not been authorized to vote (however, days later, the New York Provincial Congress endorsed the Declaration).

JOHN HANCOCK WAS the first to sign the Declaration of Independence, which was considered an act of treason against King George III of England. It's rumored that he practiced writing his name prior to affixing his famous signature rather boldly to the historic document, spawning the expression about leaving one's "John Hancock."

THE MAGNA CARTA was a thirteenth-century English legal document on which the United States based much of its original laws. England's powerful barons forced King John to grant a charter limiting his powers. The Magna Carta helped establish the principle that no one—not even a king—is above the law.

WITH THE DECLARATION of Independence in place, the United States of America was born in Philadelphia's State House (now Independence Hall).

WASHINGTON

REVOLUTION REIGNS

The early French and English settlers disputed boundaries and territories throughout the vast Ohio Valley region between the Appalachian Mountains and the Mississippi River. In many respects, the French and Indian War set the stage for the American Revolution. The French suffered a humiliating defeat, and as a result, the French would do almost anything to take revenge against the British, even if the French monarchy could not afford public financial support of American causes, which angered the British further.

Many of the dictates set forth by Great Britain on the American colonies served as a prelude to war, there's some debate as to which issues were the most pressing. Certainly, the signers of the Declaration of Independence insisted it was about liberty and democracy. Yet some modern historians argue that the Revolution was fought for money and trade.

With tensions building up between the British and the colonies, something had to give, and inside this chapter, you'll learn all about the interesting facts and stories that contributed to the revolt, which had most likely given King George more than a few sleepless nights.

UPON HIS APPOINTMENT as commander of the colonial forces, General Washington organized militia companies. Because he had fought alongside the British in the French and Indian War, he knew the contempt the British military showed for colonial officers. It didn't hurt that as a Virginian, he might bind the southern colonies to the New England patriots. If there was to be victory, Washington knew it would take all thirteen colonies working together.

———————— ★ ————————

BATTLES WERE ALREADY underway when Washington appeared at the Second Continental Congress in May 1775, dressed in his uniform of the Fairfax County militia. On June 25, 1775, Washington set out for Massachusetts to take command of the forces. Under great adversity, Washington took what was more or less an armed mob and assembled it into the Continental army with one goal: victory.

———————— ★ ————————

WASHINGTON SOUGHT LONGER terms of enlistment from Congress as well as better pay for his troops. But a leery Congress, afraid of moving from one military dictatorship to another, was not easily convinced. So Washington was forced to do the best he could under the circumstances. Considering the problems of troop defection, insubordination, lack of discipline, and a shortage of gunpowder, it's understandable that Washington maintained order at times by flogging troops, or worse. Deserters and repeat offenders were often hanged.

———————— ★ ————————

WHEN WASHINGTON FIRST took command, there was much strategic planning. On May 10, 1775, at the start of the Revolutionary War, Ethan Allen, an American Revolutionary soldier, led his Green Mountain Boys in an attack to overtake Fort Ticonderoga. These soldiers from Vermont seized the fort and all of its valuable artillery stores without a struggle. They then dragged fifty heavy cannons by sled from Fort Ticonderoga in northern New York to Boston. An astute Washington had the cannons mounted on Dorchester Heights, which commanded the city. Of course, British general William Howe saw this and fled by sea to Halifax, Nova Scotia, where he awaited the reinforcement of German mercenaries from Europe. This brought a much-needed reprieve from the occupation of any British troops in the colonies.

BRITAIN'S CLEAR ADVANTAGE was its navy, for the Americans did not have one. Sensing the final break even before the Declaration of Independence was signed, in June of 1776 the British sent General Howe to assemble his forces as well as a huge fleet. Howe landed on Long Island, pushing his way to New York City with an army of 30,000 soldiers—more than twice as many men as Washington had.

TRYING TO COPE with Howe's mighty force, Washington committed a tactical blunder that nearly cost him the war. He split his troops between Brooklyn, Long Island, and Manhattan Island. This weakened the overall American position. By the end of August, the Americans had to retreat to their Brooklyn Heights fortifications.

DURING THE REVOLUTION, when General William Howe and his British forces occupied New York City, they placed an enormous demand on the milk and cream products coming from Long Island. Long Islanders were forced to substitute tomatoes and water broth for the cream in their chowder Therefore, the proper name for red clam chowder would be Long Island clam chowder, rather than Manhattan clam chowder, as it is called.

THINKING HE HAD Washington's men cornered, Howe called off his redcoats temporarily while he planned a potential siege. This proved to be a mistake. Surrender was not on Washington's mind. Though he had no navy to rely on, the undeterred general rounded up every seaworthy vessel he could find and obtained assistance from the experienced boatmen of Marblehead, Massachusetts. In the midst of a raging storm and a thick fog, he and his men rowed across the East River to safety in Manhattan, losing not one man in his command. But although this served as a brilliant escape, it also meant that an important American seaport had been lost to the British.

A FEW DAYS after Howe landed in Manhattan, a mysterious fire leveled much of the town. Was it mere coincidence? Some have attributed it to a patriot arsonist, but whatever the fire's origin, it aided the American cause.

WASHINGTON WITHDREW HIS troops for a while, retreating to Harlem Heights, then to White Plains. The British prevailed at a White Plains skirmish. While they allowed Washington's forces to retreat in good order, the British turned their attention south, capturing Fort Washington and Fort Lee on the New Jersey shore just days later.

IN THREE MONTHS, Washington had lost New York and Long Island, and his army of 19,000 was reduced to fewer than 3,500. Desertion among the troops was rampant, and Washington was facing criticism for his performance. The circumstances became so grim that General Howe declared victory. Even the Congress fled Philadelphia for Baltimore. Washington led his contingent across the Delaware River into the relative safety of Pennsylvania. As a precaution, he ordered all boats along the New Jersey side of the river to go with them.

WASHINGTON CALLED ON the Marblehead fishermen's tactical aid once again as he launched a surprise attack on Howe's sleeping soldiers on the morning of December 26. He was fairly certain that these foreign troops, celebrating the holidays away from home, would imbibe heavily, and that this was the optimal moment to attack. Washington gained serious ground by killing, wounding, or capturing every one of the Hessian soldiers while suffering only six casualties among his men. James Monroe was one of the four wounded.

---★---

WHEN THE BRITISH hanged Nathan Hale for being a spy on September 22, 1776, he uttered the famous line, "I only regret that I have but one life to lose for my country." His words might have been inspired by a passage from Joseph Addison's play, *Cato*: "What pity is it that we can die but once to serve our country."

---★---

WASHINGTON SLIPPED PAST Trenton in the night and attacked the British the next morning. The Americans not only were victorious on the battlefield, but also were able to acquire much-needed supplies. In fact, the British felt so alarmed and threatened that they evacuated most New Jersey garrisons. With victories in the Battle of Trenton and the Battle of Princeton, and with Philadelphia no longer in peril, Washington moved north to winter quarters in Morristown, New Jersey. There, Washington turned his attention to recruitment.

---★---

THE BRITISH DIDN'T use their time wisely, for they spent the first six months of 1777 on skirmishes in northern New Jersey. General John Burgoyne felt that by striking down the Hudson River, he would cut off New England and New York from the rest of the colonies and end the colonial rebellion. After recapturing Fort Ticonderoga, Burgoyne headed toward Fort Edward. When the patriots saw them approaching, they scattered into the woods for cover, but continued to attack from behind their shield of trees. The end result was British losses of close to 1,000 men. This slowed the British down, and by the time they reached Saratoga, New York, the Americans were ready.

★

AMERICAN GENERAL HORATIO GATES positioned his troops to overlook the road to Albany so that when Burgoyne came along, he pretty much had to fight. After losing even more soldiers, Burgoyne did what he swore he'd never do—he surrendered on October 17, 1777.

★

THOUGH SARATOGA HAD turned the war in America's favor, Washington still had his struggles. Trying to protect the capital of Philadelphia, he lost the Battles of Brandywine and Germantown, and he withdrew his besieged forces to nearby Valley Forge, the site of his winter encampment.

★

WITHIN SIX MONTHS, the Continental army was ready once more. The last major battle in the northeast occurred at Monmouth in June 1778, when the British general Sir Henry Clinton, who took over as commander in chief after Howe retired, pulled troops out of Philadelphia and moved them north toward New York.

★

WASHINGTON'S ARMY CAUGHT up with them at Monmouth, New Jersey, where General Washington ordered his second in command, Charles Lee, to attack the rear of the British forces. Lee, disliking Washington's plan, fought halfheartedly and ordered retreat. This infuriated General Washington. He rallied the troops to follow his command, and Clinton's army fell back some before withdrawing to New York. Washington had once again restored sagging morale, and Lee, while trying to clear his name of wrongdoing, was court-martialed and suspended from command. When he refused to accept this, Lee was removed from the Continental army altogether.

WHILE THE ENGLISH major general John Burgoyne was fighting in the north, Howe loaded his troops aboard approximately 250 ships and sailed up the Chesapeake Bay for Philadelphia, leaving Burgoyne to face potential disaster. Washington didn't exactly expect to keep Howe out of the city. Nonetheless, he couldn't just hand it to him. Thus, he fought with an outnumbered army. The Battle of Brandywine occurred in September 1777 and was followed by the Battle of Germantown, where the British outflanked the entrenched Continental army.

ON OCTOBER 4, 1777, Howe took Philadelphia, the American capital (though government leaders had previously fled). This might have impressed the British, but it didn't do much for the French, who were beginning to take notice of the American victories in other battles.

AT THE OUTSET of the Revolution, the Americans realized their limitations. All the resources seemed to lie across the ocean. Benjamin Franklin was dispatched to France to foster financial support as well as troops. Franklin's diplomatic prowess certainly succeeded, but the victories, especially at Saratoga, spoke volumes. After seeing proof that the Continental army was a capable fighting force, and upon hearing rumors that Britain might offer America territorial concessions to reach peace, the French government ministers had enough confidence in General Washington to recommend to King Louis XVI that he sign a treaty of alliance with the Americans. In February 1778, this alliance was made formal, with France diplomatically recognizing "the United States of America." Soon after the signing, Spain, which had offered to remain neutral if Britain returned Gibraltar, threw in support, since its demands were not met. Spain and France were already allies as well.

————————— ★ —————————

FRENCH AID WAS certainly welcome, but French egos were not. Many of the officers who arrived in the summer of 1777 demanded exalted rank and commensurate pay for their limited military experience. An exception was the young Marquis de Lafayette, who arrived in Philadelphia volunteering to serve on America's behalf at his own expense. This quickly won Washington's praise and admiration from American troops.

————————— ★ —————————

LAFAYETTE HAD BEEN rushed into battle at Brandywine, and by December he had his own command and commission as a major general. In 1779, Lafayette returned to his native country to continue lobbying for further aid, thus proving to be a valuable liaison between the Continental army and the French government.

————————— ★ —————————

AMERICAN FRONTIERSMEN CONTINUED to settle, and their numbers in the region grew. This was significant because Britain had forbidden the American colonists to move beyond the Appalachians. In fact, Great

Britain had recruited Native Americans as allies to attack any western colonial settlements. But George Rogers Clark, a Virginian, seized British forts along the frontier in 1778 and braved the Ohio River. By spring 1779, he arrived in the Illinois territory.

———————— ★ ————————

GRADUALLY, THE REAL action in the war had shifted south to Virginia, the Carolinas, and Georgia, states that were home to the crucial export crops of tobacco, rice, and indigo, making the southern states perhaps the most valuable of the rebel states.

———————— ★ ————————

WHEN GEORGIA WAS founded as a British royal colony in 1733, it was illegal to owe money that you couldn't pay. People in England often went to jail until they could pay their debts. Georgia's founder, James Oglethorpe, thought that one way to help people in this position was to offer to send them to a colony in America, rather than send them to a jail in England, where they couldn't pay off their debt because they weren't free to work. And so Georgia (named for George II, the English king at the time) was born.

———————— ★ ————————

IN 1779, THE British general Cornwallis had 5,000 troops stationed in the south with the goal of forcing the "king's obedience" into the Carolinas. Loyalist sentiment was stronger here. The British secretly hoped that southern Loyalists would provide support as well as much-needed supplies.

———————— ★ ————————

IN THE AUTUMN of 1778, a large British force sailed from New York to launch a sea assault against Savannah, Georgia. The city fell to the British in December. Augusta, Georgia, fell one month later. When the French joined forces to counter the assault, they were shot to tatters. By the end of 1779, most of Georgia was firmly under British and Loyalist control.

———————— ★ ————————

WHILE CHARLESTON, SOUTH CAROLINA, had fended off attack for nearly three years, the city's defenses slowly deteriorated. The British besieged Charleston, cutting off supplies, and in May the Americans were forced to surrender. The patriots lost many military supplies in the process.

———————— ★ ————————

GREAT BRITAIN, THE world's leading maritime power, hardly feared the infant colonial navy. The British ships plied coastal waters, supplying the redcoats with whatever was needed, including more of His Majesty's troops. Still, the small patriot navy won a few surprising victories, such as when a small American squadron captured the port of Nassau in the Bahamas.

———————— ★ ————————

FARTHER OUT AT SEA, American naval power did far better, capturing some British ships and cargo. Continental navy captains—the likes of John Paul Jones from Scotland, Joshua Barney, and Irishman John Barry—proved to be heroic at sea. John Paul Jones is by far the most famous Revolutionary naval hero. In 1778, Jones raided the port of Whitehaven in England and then captured the British sloop called the *Drake*. On September 23, 1779, when the British attacked his converted merchant ship the *Bonhomme Richard* and demanded his surrender, Jones answered with the famous words, "I have not yet begun to fight!"

———————— ★ ————————

THE *AMERICAN TURTLE* submarine was launched in the dark of night on September 6–7, 1776, against the British flagship, HMS *Eagle*, which was moored in New York harbor. The submarine crew attempted to attach a bomb to the rudder of the British ship. While the *American Turtle* failed to destroy its target, the British recognized the threat and moved the fleet.

BY 1781, THERE were more than 450 privately owned vessels that had received commissions to attack British shipping. And although these did not impede the British troops and their supply provisions, they added tremendous cost to the war Britain waged.

Thanks to the French navy, Britain's supremacy was sufficiently threatened, and the war at sea saw fewer American defeats with added victories. French naval forces fought off the Virginia coast, successfully trapping the British general Cornwallis and his army.

THE REVOLUTIONARY WAR had raged for six years when, in the summer of 1781, the second French fleet arrived. Washington had sent General Lafayette to confront Cornwallis near the Chesapeake Bay. There, the British were awaiting supplies from New York. But upon hearing of the French fleet, Washington changed plans, leaving New York himself and heading south.

WASHINGTON COORDINATED THE land and sea operation that brought the final climax of the war. First, the French fleet blockaded Yorktown early that September, followed by a combined Franco-American army that Washington commanded. The troops took up siege positions on land and by early October had trapped the British against the York River. In a gross misjudgment, Cornwallis had his back to the sea. Daily he endured gunfire and continual pounding from the cannons until he was forced to ask the Americans for terms of surrender on October 17, 1781. Two days later, the once mighty (and haughty) British army paraded its units between the victorious French and American soldiers, laying down their arms, while a British band played the popular tune "The World Turned Upside Down."

———————— ★ ————————

UNABLE TO CONCEDE the war, Cornwallis sent a representative, General O'Hara, to surrender his sword. General O'Hara approached a French commander, who indicated that the sword should go to General Washington. However, Washington felt that an officer of equal rank should receive it. Thus, his second in command, Major General Benjamin Lincoln, received the British sword in surrender.

———————— ★ ————————

BACK IN ENGLAND, King George III was prepared to fight on, but the British Parliament put an end to that notion. It had taken more than six years of war, and skirmishes before that, to drive its greatest overseas possession toward independence. In February 1782, Lord North's ministry in Britain fell. Parliament would no longer support a war in America.

———————— ★ ————————

THE FIRST PURPLE HEART, a military decoration awarded to those wounded or killed in action, was designed by General Washington and established in 1782. One of his creative ways to keep his soldiers fighting on when the pay envelopes were not forthcoming was to grant a commission and promote men in rank. Winners of this Purple Heart would be permitted to pass any Continental guards or sentries without challenge.

———————— ★ ————————

GENERAL WASHINGTON COULD have easily usurped power and taken the role of a military dictator, or perhaps become a king himself. Instead, he chose the route of obedience to the Continental Congress and worked tirelessly to establish a strong central government by and for the people. Not only did Washington stress the need for a Constitutional Convention, he presided over it and helped gain ratification of the Constitution of the United States.

PEACE WAS OFFICIALLY proclaimed on April 15, 1783, but it wasn't until November that the last British boats left. The formal signing of the Peace of Paris occurred in September 1783, nearly two years after Cornwallis's surrender at Yorktown. Though Britain had hoped to give the Americans less than complete independence, it finally did just that, recognizing the thirteen United States of America.

ON DECEMBER 4, 1783, Washington took leave of his principal officers at New York City's Fraunces Tavern. He'd enjoyed the sweet taste of victory several times, but had also swallowed a few bitter defeats. The general had also pacified his former officers, many of whom had not been paid what they'd been promised. He implored these impatient patriots to back down from their threats of military takeover. As he relinquished command, he pledged further service to his new country to "the utmost of my abilities."

SEEKING A QUIET life, Washington returned home to his estate at Mount Vernon in Virginia. En route, he stopped at Annapolis, Maryland, where Congress was meeting, to surrender his commission as commander in chief. But in the months and years that followed, others would hold him to his pledge of service.

CHAPTER 3

THE
NEW NATION

Among the fifty-five delegates who gathered in Philadelphia for four scorching months in the summer of 1787 were merchants, planters, landlords, and other men of wealth and prestige. Some owned slaves and some did not. There were famous war generals and outspoken patriots. All assembled to carve out the Constitution, and little did they know that the entire process from debate and drafting to signing and ratification would take more than a year. While you probably know the basics surrounding the start of our nation, this chapter will show you that there's always more to learn about our founding fathers and the start of our country.

THE ARTICLES OF Confederation, which had governed the United States, were simple. They were good for the war effort, but too limited to guide the new nation down its fought-for path of independence. There was no governor, no chief executive, and no court to interpret the law. Each state had one vote, regardless of its population. The Congress had military and diplomatic power but could not levy taxes to pay for any of it. It couldn't regulate commerce. Any shift in power, or any change at all, required unanimous consent of the states.

UNDER THE ARTICLES of Confederation, Congress could do little without the consent of the affected states. The memory of an oppressive monarch was still quite fresh. George Washington saw this as a sign of weakness and disorganization.

WHEN A GROUP of debt-ridden farmers led an insurrection against Massachusetts (called the Shays's Rebellion), Washington grew alarmed and feared that the eight years of bloodshed and expense invested in the United States would be wasted unless some better structure was brought forth.

THE U.S. CONSTITUTION came after the Articles of Confederation, which were ratified between the years of 1777 and 1781. Years later, discussions to modify them led to the creation of the Constitution, transforming the loose confederation of colonies into the United States of America.

THE LAND ORDINANCE of 1785 provided for the surrendering of state-claimed lands to the national government for orderly division and sale. The concept of public education started with the 1785 Land Ordinance, as one section of each thirty-six-square-mile area was set aside for a school and teacher.

THE NORTHWEST ORDINANCE of 1787 had extraordinary provisions that would be carried on in the Constitution, including protection of choice of religion (including none at all), habeas corpus, trial by jury, bail release, and basic due process. It went further to make guarantees to Native Americans and finally establish a system for the application for statehood. Finally, the government plan under the Articles of Confederation negotiated the peace settlement at the end of the American Revolution.

DELEGATES FROM ALL states, with the exception of Rhode Island, converged on Philadelphia in May 1787 to revise the Articles of Confederation. The legislature unanimously chose Washington as president of the convention, and most agreed on a few prevailing principles once Alexander Hamilton convinced the crowd that the Articles had best be scrapped and another document created.

THE THIRTEEN ORIGINAL states admitted were Delaware, Pennsylvania, New Jersey, Georgia, Connecticut, Massachusetts, Maryland, South Carolina, New Hampshire, Virginia, New York, North Carolina, and Rhode Island.

DELAWARE WAS THE first of the original thirteen colonies that won their independence from England to ratify the U.S. Constitution.

WHEN MISSOURI WAS ready to become a state, it turned out that it was a few thousand people short of the number required to become a state. So Congress shaved off what we now call the "bootheel" from the Arkansas Territory, and added it to Missouri in order to make its population high enough to qualify it for statehood.

GEORGE WASHINGTON LED the delegates, which included Benjamin Franklin, Alexander Hamilton, and James Madison. In Europe on diplomatic matters, Thomas Jefferson and John Adams missed the work and the rancor. Patrick Henry, who supported the limited central government of the Confederation, staunchly refused to attend.

NEW JERSEY'S WILLIAM Paterson proposed reforming the Articles of Confederation, thus allowing the Confederation to levy taxes and regulate commerce and trade. His New Jersey Plan would recognize congressional acts as supreme beyond the laws of the respective states. However, the convention rejected Paterson's plan.

JAMES MADISON, representing Virginia, presented his alternative for a national republic with a powerful central government, which limited the sovereignty of individual states. Madison's Virginia Plan drew its authority not from the thirteen states but from the population as a whole. The convention voted to accept the Virginia Plan, with its idea of a lower house based on population, and left a committee to work out the composition of the upper house.

ON JULY 16, 1787, the committee proposed the "Great Compromise" that each state have two members in this upper house of legislative government. As part of this concept, there was a three-part national government with lower and upper houses, an executive branch, and a judiciary component chosen by the entire legislature.

WHILE THE DELEGATES agreed to the basic principles that Madison and his Virginia Plan outlined early in June, they began to address contentious topics, including this issue of population in regard to representation, as well as regional issues such as slavery.

MORAL ARGUMENTS OVER the practice of slavery entered into the convention's debate. The delegates compromised, and the Constitution permitted slaves to be imported until 1808, when Congress could ban slave importation and trade. Northerners reluctantly agreed to the Fugitive Slave Clause that allowed owners to reclaim runaway slaves who fled to other states.

MANY SOUTHERN STATES had large numbers of black slaves, and Northern delegates argued that since slaves could not vote, they should not be counted for purposes of representation. Doing so would yield more power to the Southern agenda. Of course, the Southerners didn't see it this way, arguing that slaves should be counted as part of the population. Compromise came when it was agreed that three-fifths of a state's enslaved populace would be counted for representation and taxation.

———————— ★ ————————

THE CONSTITUTION REQUIRED more work when it came to defining judicial power. The delegates created a Supreme Court and left the rest of the planning to the first Congress, which then had to tackle how this court system would be established. Having accepted the "Great Compromise," they agreed that the Senate would be the governmental body filled with two delegates from each state, and that the House of Representatives would be based on population in those states. In addition, rather than have the people vote for the president and vice president, they would select members of a small Electoral College to do so. In the event that one candidate did not receive a majority of votes cast by this Electoral College, the House of Representatives was charged with making the selection.

———————— ★ ————————

THE UNITED STATES CONSTITUTION says that in order for a person to serve as president, he or she must be: (1) a "natural born citizen" of the United States; (2) at least thirty-five years old; and (3) a resident of the United States for at least fourteen years. A "natural born citizen" is anyone who was born in the United States or in any place that is considered United States property, such as the grounds of any U.S. embassy overseas or what used to be the United States Canal Zone in Panama.

———————— ★ ————————

THE ENTIRE CONSTITUTION is displayed at the National Archives in Washington, DC, only once a year on September 17, the anniversary of the date on which it was signed. On other days, the first and fourth pages are displayed in a bulletproof case. At night they are lowered into a vault strong enough to withstand a nuclear explosion!

THE EXECUTIVE OFFICE would be responsible for carrying out all laws, and the executive officer, the president, would serve as commander in chief of the armed forces. In addition, the president would oversee foreign relations and appoint federal judges and other federal officials.

REGARDING ISSUES OF finance, the delegates gave the power of currency issue to the new national government. This took away from the individual states the right to issue money. The power of taxation was given to both the national and the state governments.

DELEGATES TO THE Constitutional Convention were astute in setting up a system of checks and balances. For instance, even though the president also served as the commander in chief, only Congress could declare war. The delegates gave the president veto power over Congress, although with a two-thirds majority, the Congress could override such an action. The judicial checks were less thought-out at this juncture, but years later, when the chief justice of the United States declared a law unconstitutional, the judicial review process became more firmly established.

ON SEPTEMBER 17, 1787, after much debate, the convention completed the Constitution of the United States. Now, the conventioneers had to gather the delegates' formal signatures, and the states had to ratify the new document outlining the new form of government. Actually, nine states had to ratify the Constitution before it would take effect. Five states—Delaware, Pennsylvania, New Jersey, Georgia, and Connecticut—were the first to approve, and New Hampshire provided the decisive ratification vote in 1788. Some states, including New York and Pennsylvania, insisted more work be done to safeguard fundamental individual rights.

CONGRESS SUBMITTED TWELVE amendments, ten of which were adopted as Articles I through X of the U.S. Constitution—collectively known as the Bill of Rights. When Congress introduced the Bill of Rights in 1789, North Carolina and Rhode Island gave their formal approval to the Constitution, which was by now already operating as the law of the land.

CIVIL RIGHTS AND civil liberties refer to the guarantees of freedom, justice, and equality for all citizens. More precisely, civil rights imply equal protection and opportunity under the law, as we know it today. Civil liberties refer to freedom of speech, press, religion, and due process of the law.

THE FIRST TEN amendments to the U.S. Constitution (ratified on December 15, 1791) form what is known as the Bill of Rights. These rights are not bestowed on the people by government, but rather they are rights that the people assume and that the government is forbidden to violate.

ONCE THE DELEGATES signed the U.S. Constitution, they returned to their respective states and set forth to see it ratified. But two factions had different notions. Antifederalists were alarmed by the Constitution's first phrase of "We the people of the United States," thinking that the Constitution might nullify the independence of the states. Antifederalists argued that too many differing agendas in large states would make it impossible for one way to prevail. They feared a strong central government, thinking that, at some point, states' rights would become null and void.

FEDERALISTS BELIEVED IN a strong central government; merchants and professionals made up this faction. The opposing party, the Antifederalists, was composed of mainly farmers, many of whom owed large debts.

THE FEDERALIST PAPERS, written by Alexander Hamilton, James Madison, and John Jay, defended the new Constitution. This trio of authors wrote under the pen name of Publius. New York newspapers ran the individual papers beginning in October 1787, and the collective work was published in 1788 in book form.

THE FEDERALIST PAPERS did influence New York's ratification, but did little else around the new nation. Only when they were analyzed later was their brilliance realized. The authors' outline of the U.S. Constitution helped others to further understand the intricacies of the nation's government.

PERHAPS MADISON'S GREATEST accomplishment was in coming up with an agreement between the smaller states and the larger states that allowed the U.S. Constitution to be passed and ratified. Without James Madison there would have been no U.S. Constitution, and America would probably be a very different place today.

---- ★ ----

THOUGH WORN OUT by battle, George Washington reluctantly accepted the call to become the first president, relinquishing his genteel retirement at Mount Vernon. Mindful that his leadership was sorely needed to unify the infant nation, he pressed for ratification of the U.S. Constitution, which he firmly believed was the best that could be written at the time. Washington was so popular that if he gave this new document and governmental creation his blessing, then others would also.

---- ★ ----

ON APRIL 30, 1789, Washington took the oath of office in the portico of Federal Hall on Wall Street, New York City. Also present were Vice President John Adams, both houses of the newly organized Congress, and an exuberant crowd of onlookers.

---- ★ ----

HIS FIRST INAUGURAL address was brief and modest, containing only one suggestion to the new Congress—that its members "would carefully avoid every alteration which might endanger the benefits of a united and effective government, or which ought to await the future lessons of experience." Washington knew there was widespread support for the original amendments that made up the Bill of Rights. He supported these, but also had the foresight to know that further attempts to amend the document too quickly would hinder the fledgling nation.

WASHINGTON WAS CAREFUL not to set precedents that would start dangerous trends toward a monarchy or dictatorship. He respected the divisions of power created in the Constitution, and he spent his first days in office listening to divergent viewpoints as he organized the executive branch. Landowners tended to have more conservative views, and as George Washington was a propertied gentleman himself, he tried to recognize the more liberal outlook of farmers and artisans who made up the majority of the population.

Congress delivered a tariff, or tax bill, to Washington in June for his signature. The measure would provide the new government a source of much-needed revenue.

★

THE ORIGINAL CABINET, which is part of the "Unwritten Constitution," consisted of only four departments: the State Department, Treasury Department, War Department, and the Office of the Attorney General. Today's cabinet consists of fifteen departments: the Departments of Agriculture, Commerce, Defense, Education, Energy, Health and Human Services, Homeland Security, Housing and Urban Development, Interior, Labor, State, Transportation, Treasury, Veterans Affairs, and the Office of the Attorney General.

★

THE ISSUE OF where to establish the permanent seat of government was postponed until the next congressional session, but by the close of the first one, bills had been passed establishing three executive departments representing the president's cabinet—State, Treasury, and War.

★

CONGRESS ALSO ESTABLISHED a federal judiciary comprising the Supreme Court of one chief justice, five associate justices, and thirteen district courts. An attorney general would be the nation's highest law officer.

IN KEEPING WITH his careful decisions, Washington chose a balance of liberals and conservatives for his cabinet. Alexander Hamilton became secretary of the treasury and Henry Knox the first secretary of war; Edmund Randolph of Virginia was offered the post of attorney general. Washington awaited the return of Thomas Jefferson, who was the U.S. diplomatic representative to France, in order to offer him the position of secretary of state. Our first president nominated John Jay of New York as chief justice of the United States.

DURING THE FIRST administration, the seat of government proposal was passed in July 1790 establishing Philadelphia as the capital until 1800, when a federal district on the Potomac would be established.

THE BILL OF Rights was approved in 1791, and President Washington also signed a bill creating the first bank of the United States. The banking issue proved to be the first test of the Constitution's flexibility. Jefferson asserted that a bank bill was unconstitutional, but Hamilton insisted that a national bank was essential.

AS THE PRESIDENT celebrated his sixtieth birthday, he wasn't exactly overjoyed that his two principal advisers—Jefferson and Hamilton—had fundamental differences. Hamilton's backers evolved into the Federalist

Party, backing a strong central government. Those supporting Jefferson for the Republican Party, which later became known as the Democratic-Republican Party, held firm to the opinion that states should have the right to decide matters relating to them.

———————— ★ ————————

THE 1792 ELECTION drew near, and Washington's close advisers unanimously agreed that times were too perilous to risk a transfer of the executive branch to anyone other than the current president. The Northern states were disagreeing with their Southern neighbors over the reapportionment of seats in the House of Representatives. Washington vetoed a plan that would have favored the North, viewing it as unconstitutional, and he grew anxious over the tendency of Northern and Southern states to part ways on political issues. Though he wanted to bid farewell to public life, Washington agreed to a second term and was the unanimous choice, along with Vice President Adams, in the 1792 election.

———————— ★ ————————

THE 1792 ELECTION started the two-term tradition that would continue until the administration of Franklin Delano Roosevelt in the 1930s. The Twenty-second Amendment codified the two-term provision when it was ratified in 1951.

———————— ★ ————————

JUST TWO WEEKS after the inauguration in March 1793, news reached Philadelphia that King Louis XVI of France had been executed, followed by news that Revolutionary France had declared war on Britain, Spain, and the Netherlands.

———————— ★ ————————

THE PROCLAMATION OF Neutrality was issued in 1793. Citizen Genêt would be received, and the earlier treaties stood, although they would be interpreted quite cautiously.

AS 1793 DREW to a close, Thomas Jefferson desired a retreat from public life. Thus, he resigned as secretary of state and was succeeded by Edmund Randolph, the attorney general (a post taken over by William Bradford from Pennsylvania).

THE DANGER OF war with Britain increased by spring 1794 as British warships seized neutral vessels trading with the French West Indies. This caused Washington to approve a thirty-day embargo on all sailing from American ports to avoid any future clashes, and it served as the impetus Congress needed to authorize the construction of six frigates, the first naval requisitions since the Revolutionary War. By signing the Jay Treaty with Great Britain, Washington allowed American ships to be inspected at sea, but the treaty also removed British troops from the Northwest Territory.

HAVING GUIDED THE new country through a war for independence and through eight years of its early government, a weary President Washington was determined to leave office and retire to Mount Vernon. It had been an eventful tenure—averting war, opening the economic gateways of the West, and proving that the Constitution did work.

In his famous Farewell Address, Washington outlined the reasons for his decision not to seek a third term. He delivered the address to his cabinet, and it was published the following day in newspapers.

THE STORY OF George Washington and the Cherry Tree states that when Washington was a boy, he chopped down a cherry tree and then told his father what he had done. It is a nice story, but a man named Parson Weems actually made up the story after Washington's death on December 14, 1799. Weems hoped that by putting such stories of Washington's honest nature into a book, he could make lots of money.

★

ANOTHER MYTH ABOUT George Washington was that he owned wooden teeth. His teeth were real teeth—they just weren't *his* teeth. In fact, they weren't even human teeth! They were made from hippopotamus ivory, and were very expensive. They were also very painful. They're one of the main reasons why we have no paintings of Washington smiling.

★

BEFORE 1776, MOST Americans (except for Pennsylvania's Quakers and Rhode Island's Baptists) lived in colonies with established churches. Independence significantly changed religious practices. Patriots who were once proud members of the Church of England repudiated their allegiance to the now-defeated king. Instead, they formed the Protestant Episcopal Church of America. In fact, in order to win support for the war in Virginia, a Declaration of Rights was passed guaranteeing religious toleration.

★

DURING THE REVOLUTIONARY War, British warships had temporarily destroyed the New England fishing industry and seized many American merchant ships. Southern states, where tobacco and rice were key exports, and even the grain regions of the North, suffered a disruption of trade following the long fight for independence.

WHEN BRITISH TROOPS had occupied port cities such as Boston, New York, Philadelphia, Charleston, and Newport, trade virtually ceased. Peace didn't bring back prewar prosperity. British merchants, angry over the war as well as unpaid debts, refused tobacco from the Chesapeake, and in South Carolina the indigo industry collapsed. American ships no longer traded with the sugar islands in the British West Indies, thanks to the British Navigation Acts. The result was a commercial recession spanning nearly two decades. By 1790, the value of American exports was a fraction of what it had been twenty years earlier, and with the standard of living in decline, America was ripe for economic conflict.

THOUGH HE WASN'T a popular war hero like his predecessor, John Adams had participated in framing the Declaration of Independence (although Jefferson was the author) and had served as a diplomat in Europe. When John Adams became our second president in 1797, Great Britain and France were at war, and to his credit, Adams kept the United States out of the conflict. In an attitude of preparedness, however, Adams did establish a naval department and ordered warships to be built. During this time, the USS *Constitution* sailed for the first time.

DURING THE NINETEENTH CENTURY, political parties were run at the local level by men called party bosses. They were rarely elected and did not answer to anyone. They could get people hired to city jobs or appointed to state or federal positions, depending on how powerful they were. These local party members became part of the political machines that the bosses ran. At the beginning of the twentieth century, people started to fight corruption in politics and party bosses and party machines began to die out.

JOHN ADAMS WAS the first American president to go to Harvard College, but he has hardly been the last. More American presidents have attended this Cambridge, Massachusetts, institution of higher learning than any other college in the country!

JOHN AND ABIGAIL ADAMS were the first president and first lady to enjoy the newly created presidential mansion as Washington, DC, became the nation's capital in 1800. Adams is reported to have written during his second night in the President's House (what would come to be known as the White House), "I pray Heaven to bestow the best Blessings on this House and all that shall hereafter inhabit it. May none but honest and wise Men ever rule under this roof."

THOMAS JEFFERSON SUCCEEDED Adams as president. He felt that "the government that governs best governs least." Indeed, he was a proponent of limited power, and a protector of individual and state rights. Jefferson is one of the most learned men in American history, with early patriot ties, diplomatic tenure abroad, and a keen interest in architecture. He spoke six languages, designed his own home at Monticello in Charlottesville, Virginia, and founded the University of Virginia.

IN 1803, JEFFERSON seized the opportunity to purchase a vast expanse of land from France for $15 million (no doubt one of the greatest real estate bargains in U.S. history), even though the Constitution did not authorize him to do so. France was willing to sell the land from Louisiana in the south to present-day Montana in the north because of the fear that it was about to fall into British hands anyway.

JEFFERSON WOUND UP receiving all of the territory that lay between the Mississippi River and Spanish Mexico for $15 million, which totals out to just three cents per acre.

IN ORDER TO pay his debts, Thomas Jefferson placed his large personal library of books up for sale. The U.S. Congress bought them as a favor to a great American, and they became the basis for the book collection we know today as the Library of Congress.

JEFFERSON SENT Meriwether Lewis and William Clark to explore the newly acquired territory. The Louisiana Purchase made westward expansion possible and effectively doubled the size of the country.

IN 1808, CONGRESS prohibited the import of slaves from Africa.

HAVING BEEN RE-ELECTED to a second term, Jefferson stepped down with the belief that no president should govern longer than eight years. He retired to Monticello, where he died on July 4, 1826.

JOHN ADAMS AND Thomas Jefferson died on the same day: the fiftieth anniversary of their greatest achievement, the Declaration of Independence. Adams's last words before he died that evening were: "Jefferson still lives." There was no way he could have known that Thomas Jefferson himself had died earlier that same day!

BURIED AT THE ESTATE, Jefferson left behind his own epitaph, which read: "Here was buried Thomas Jefferson, Author of the Declaration of Independence, of the Statute of Virginia for Religious Freedom, and the Father of the University of Virginia." He chose to leave out the detail of being the nation's third president.

AMERICA'S GROWING PAINS

When James Madison *took office in 1809, he was already well known for his contributions to the Bill of Rights. Much of Madison's presidency was filled with continued tension with foreign governments. The Embargo Act of 1807, prohibiting U.S. vessels from trading with European nations and passed by Congress over Federalist opposition, seriously harmed the U.S. economy and was replaced two years later with the Non-Intercourse Act, which forbade trade with France and Great Britain. You'll explore all the struggles—some well-known, others rarely spoken of—this country had in its early stages in this entertaining chapter.*

BY 1810, MADISON realized the American trade boycott was having little effect, for both countries continued seizing American ships. The Non-Intercourse Act was repealed in May 1810, but Madison was ready to prohibit trade again, if necessary. U.S.–British relations worsened as a result of these maritime troubles and also because of America's expansion into British-held lands in the West, in Canada, and in Florida (Spanish-held at the time).

★

IN NOVEMBER 1811, Governor William Henry Harrison of Indiana fought the Shawnee nation with American troops at the Battle of Tippecanoe. Though the president had not authorized the use of troops, the incident roused support for military preparedness as war with Britain looked probable.

★

BY THE SPRING of 1812, Madison urged Britain to revoke trade restrictions. Great Britain ignored the requests, and Madison asked Congress to place an embargo, implying that even stronger measures might be warranted against the country.

★

THE BRITISH, AT war with France's Napoleon, had a pressing need to increase the ranks of the Royal Navy. They boarded U.S. vessels and impressed American sailors into His Majesty's service. Adding to the turmoil, a congressional faction dubbed the "War Hawks" viewed war with Britain as potential relief from the Native American hostilities Great Britain had backed, and also as a means of further expansion in Spanish Florida, since Spain was allied with Britain in the battles against Napoleon.

★

AT THE HARTFORD Convention in December of 1814, New England Federalist representatives supported the doctrine of states' rights in declaring that a state had the right to oppose and not abide by congressional actions.

ON JUNE 19, Madison signed a declaration of war, passed by both houses of Congress. What wasn't known, however, was that Britain had actually revoked the practice of intercepting American ships a few days prior, and apparently the French had repealed their own restrictions on American trade.

MADISON'S CALL FOR preparedness had not been heeded, and the country was ill prepared for war. This brought only ridicule to the administration that had already heard the Northern and Southern differences of opinion. Northerners showed no interest in annexing Florida, a Southern conquest, and Southerners saw any move into Canada as strength added to the Northern states. New England Federalists called the War of 1812 "Mr. Madison's War."

THE AMERICAN FLAG flying over Fort McHenry at daybreak inspired Francis Scott Key to write "The Star-Spangled Banner" in 1814. Key had boarded a British frigate under a flag of truce to arrange a prisoner's release, and scrawled the poem on a handbill. Later set to the tune of an infamous English drinking song, it officially became the national anthem on March 13, 1931.

ALTHOUGH THE U.S. NAVY won several victories in the war's first year, 1813 saw the British navy seize many ports and capture several American ships. One American vessel—the USS *Constitution*—had earned a reputation for getting the best of British ships. In August 1812, it had sighted the British warship *Guerrière* sailing close enough that the *Constitution* could open fire, essentially shredding *Guerrière*'s sails and rendering her dead at sea. After demolishing the ship, the *Constitution* sailed to Brazilian waters, turning the HMS *Java* into a flaming ruin. With all the heavy fire she weathered, the *Constitution* was quickly dubbed "Old Ironsides."

---------- ★ ----------

BATTLES WERE FOUGHT along the Great Lakes and into the Canadian frontier. The Battle of Lake Erie, under Oliver Perry's command, was the turning point in the northwest for the Americans and tipped the balance of power. Around the time that Key wrote his poem, both American and British negotiators were meeting in Belgium to agree on settlement terms. But while peace was being procured, the British decided to invade the Gulf Coast.

---------- ★ ----------

ANDREW JACKSON WON a decisive victory over the British in the Battle of New Orleans on January 8, 1815. This was perhaps the greatest (and most unnecessary) battle of the War of 1812. News of peace and the Treaty of Ghent finally reached Jackson in March, months after the final resolution had been agreed upon on December 24, 1814. The treaty essentially restored matters to prewar conditions. Neither side left the war with more territory than it had commenced fighting with, though the United States claimed victory.

---------- ★ ----------

AN UNFORTUNATE OUTCOME of the war resulted in the British taking the city of Washington, DC, and burning many government buildings, including the president's home, referred to as the White House. The British saw this torching as justifiable retaliation for the American burning of York (now Toronto), the capital of Upper Canada, the previous year.

WHEN DOLLEY MADISON was warned that the British were en route and was told to flee the White House, she calmly collected the president's papers, the national seal, and the Gilbert Stuart portrait of George Washington, and sent them off for safekeeping. Her actions earned her a reputation as the plucky first lady who kept her head in a crisis.

ON AUGUST 24, 1814, President Madison joined his armies in retreating from the nation's capital. Three days later, he returned to the burnt rubble the British had left behind.

PRESIDENT MADISON ORDERED the Presidential Mansion to be whitewashed, or painted white, as part of the repairs needed to restore it. It has been painted white ever since, and that's why it's now called the White House.

THE 1783 CONGRESS decided that the nation's capital would move from Philadelphia in 1800. After much debate, members passed the Residence Act, which outlined a ten-miles-square site on the Potomac River along the Virginia–Maryland border, an area that President George Washington had selected.

PRESIDENT JOHN ADAMS was the first leader to govern from Federal City, later named Washington, DC, in honor of our nation's first president. Today, the city of Washington exists as the District of Columbia (DC), the federal district of the United States, named after Christopher Columbus.

———————— ★ ————————

WHILE THE AREA was being surveyed, Washington and Thomas Jefferson selected French architect Pierre L'Enfant to design the city, which, at the time it was surveyed, included Georgetown (Maryland) and Alexandria (Virginia). L'Enfant's plan featured broad avenues radiating out from Capitol Hill, interrupted by a series of rectangular and circular parks, all overlaid with a perpendicular grid of streets. The grid was then slashed with diagonal avenues named for the thirteen original states.

———————— ★ ————————

THE FRENCH ARCHITECT began supervising construction, but he lacked a cost-containment attitude. After his many quarrels with public officials, he was dismissed in 1792. L'Enfant died in poverty in 1825, but appreciation of his architectural vision grew in later generations. Over the years, most of his ideas were realized.

———————— ★ ————————

SINCE THE DISTRICT OF COLUMBIA is a federal district and not a state, the inhabitants originally had no real local government, and they had no vote in federal elections. The ratification of the Twenty-third Amendment in 1961 gave Washington, DC, three electoral votes, so its population could participate in the election of the president and vice president.

———————— ★ ————————

WHEN THE GOVERNMENT transfer took effect in 1800, the town boasted fewer than 5,000 people. Of course, the British burning of important buildings (including the White House) in 1814 did much to halt early growth.

IN 1847, THE part of the district that lies on the Potomac's western banks was returned to Virginia, and today Washington, DC, covers only about two-thirds its original size. The residential population grew to approximately 52,000 by 1850, and then increased dramatically, reaching 132,000 by 1870.

THE BRITISH INDEED used the fighting power of Native Americans in the War of 1812. William Henry Harrison fought the Shawnee nation at the Battle of Tippecanoe while Andrew Jackson commanded the Tennessee militia winning the Battle of Horseshoe Bend. The Treaty of Fort Jackson in 1814 signaled the end of Native American supremacy in Mississippi.

FOLLOWING THE WAR OF 1812, Native Americans were moved to lands west of Mississippi, commonly referred to as "Indian Territory." Although removal had gone on since the early 1800s, the Indian Removal Act of 1830, implemented during Andrew Jackson's presidency, resulted in the uprooting of entire tribes from their homelands.

As some Native Americans refused to resettle, several smaller wars or skirmishes ensued. The Black Hawk War in Illinois and Wisconsin was one of these, ending in 1832.

ATTEMPTS BY THE Cherokees to stop the removal from their homes brought them to the Supreme Court. In Cherokee Nation v. Georgia (1831), the Supreme Court ruled that the Cherokees could remain on their land, and in Worcester v. Georgia (1832), the Supreme Court once again backed the rights of the Cherokees. Andrew Jackson refused to enforce the Court's decision. Although impeachment proceedings were started in the House of Representatives, they failed to go very far. From 1835 to 1838, the forced march known as the Trail of Tears resulted in the deaths of thousands of Cherokees.

THE REMAINING CREEK were uprooted from Mississippi and Alabama, and the Seminole fought to resist the U.S. Army's attempts to force their retreat from Florida. By the end of the 1850s, only scattered groups of Native Americans remained in the eastern United States.

AS THE 1820s APPROACHED, the young nation was about to announce its first major position on foreign policy. The stability of the Western Hemisphere was being threatened by European events, most notably Spain's intention to reclaim as colonies the Latin American states that had recently gained their independence. In 1823 in his seventh annual message to Congress, President Monroe set forth his opinion that no European nation should attempt to further colonize in the Western Hemisphere, and that they shouldn't interfere with the newly independent Spanish-American republics. He added that the United States would not interfere with existing European colonies or in the European continent itself. This became known as the Monroe Doctrine.

AT THE TIME, the United States did not possess the naval power to enforce these sentiments, but the Monroe Doctrine would be used in future generations to justify American occupation of Haiti, the Dominican Republic, and Nicaragua in order to protect them from foreign influence. The Monroe Doctrine remains part of the foreign policy of the United States today.

JAMES MONROE, THE last of the presidents who participated in the American Revolution as an adult, died on the Fourth of July in 1831. This was exactly five years after both Thomas Jefferson and John Adams died!

ON MARCH 9, 1820, President Monroe's younger daughter, Maria, became the first White House bride. She was the first relative of a president to be married in what Americans then called the Executive Mansion. There have been many White House weddings since.

JOHN QUINCY ADAMS, son of the nation's second president, followed James Monroe into the highest office. A scholarly man, he found citizens not quite as willing to allot their tax dollars to specific advancements he deemed important, including new roads and canals, along with scientific exploration.

FROM THOMAS JEFFERSON to John Quincy Adams (four in a row), every president had previously been secretary of state. In fact, Madison, Monroe, and Adams all went from being secretary of state directly to being president. Adams was the last one to do this though.

ADAMS SERVED ONLY four years in office, though he went on to a distinguished career as a member of the House of Representatives, where he was a vigorous opponent of slavery. In 1848, at the age of eighty, John Quincy Adams suffered a stroke while fulfilling his House duties, and died days later.

—————— ★ ——————

THE 363-MILE-LONG ERIE CANAL, which opened the West to commerce, proved to be an engineering marvel as well as a grand commercial success. Completed in 1825, this artificial inland waterway extended from Lake Erie, at Buffalo, New York, to the Hudson River, near Albany. With increased commerce, New York City grew to become the nation's leading financial and commercial center.

—————— ★ ——————

ANDREW JACKSON, known for his heroic battlefield experiences in the Battle of New Orleans, took office as the seventh president in 1829. He served two terms, resulting from his popularity with voters. Jackson saw himself as a champion of the average citizen, continually battling Congress and vetoing legislation he thought favored the wealthy elite. Thus, his policies became known as "Jacksonian Democracy."

—————— ★ ——————

WHILE HE SAW himself as average, Andrew Jackson's home, the Hermitage, was one of the finest mansions in America during its day.

—————— ★ ——————

ANDREW JACKSON FOUGHT many duels during his lifetime. One particular duel in 1806 (fought over an insult to Jackson's wife) left Jackson with a bullet lodged so close to his heart that it could never be removed. Amazingly, Jackson had the second shot in this duel and killed his opponent.

MARTIN VAN BUREN, Jackson's vice president, succeeded him in 1837. Unfortunately, the nation was mired in an economic recession, and Van Buren never did find the cure voters sought. Thus, they voted him out of office, and William Henry Harrison was inaugurated in 1841.

MARTIN VAN BUREN was the first president of the United States to be born after the American Revolution, and so he was the first president to be born as an American citizen. The men who served as president before him were all British subjects when they were born.

OVER THE YEARS many presidential candidates have done their best to show voters that they are just ordinary folks, and none was more successful at doing this than William Henry Harrison. Harrison ran for president by emphasizing his humble origins on the frontier. While it's true that Harrison was born in a log cabin, the whole truth is that the log cabin in which he was born was a temporary home around which his father's mansion was being built.

HARRISON'S FATHER HAD signed the Declaration of Independence, and the president himself earned military recognition at the Battle of Tippecanoe, defeating Shawnee warriors in the Indiana Territory. But alas, Harrison never got to prove himself in office, as one month after his inauguration, he died of pneumonia. He is now known as the president who served the shortest term.

JOHN TYLER BECAME the first vice president to succeed to the presidency. Though a Whig, he departed from party projects such as a national bank and federally funded roads and canals. Worse yet, he supported slavery, making him an outcast in his own political party. It was no surprise that he served only one term. James Polk won election in 1845.

———————— ★ ————————

JOHN TYLER WAS married twice during his seventy-one years. During that time he had fifteen children. President Tyler's last child was born in 1860 when Tyler was seventy years old.

———————— ★ ————————

THE TERM DARK HORSE CANDIDATE originally came from an 1831 English novel in which an unknown horse came out of the back of the pack to win a horse race. By the 1840s it had become a political term that referred to someone who wasn't well known coming out of nowhere to win a political contest. James K. Polk of Tennessee was the first dark horse candidate to win the presidency.

———————— ★ ————————

PRESIDENT JAMES K. POLK laid the cornerstone—or the first stone—for the Washington Monument on July 4, 1848. The building project ran into budget problems when the monument was half completed, and work on it stopped for decades. It wasn't completed until 1888. Now, the bottom half of the structure is a slightly different color of marble than the top half is. The forty years it took to finish the monument are the reason for this difference.

———————— ★ ————————

THE IDEA OF Manifest Destiny—that the United States had the God-given right to expand across the North American continent—was a popular and fervently held belief in the mid-1800s. The idea justified taking Native American territory, and it incited claims to even more land.

MEXICO, WHICH HAD just won its independence from Spain, had originally encouraged U.S. settlers in Texas, but its dictator, General Antonio López de Santa Anna, later banned further U.S. immigration. And when Texas declared its own independence from Mexico in 1836, Santa Anna marched to San Antonio with a force of 3,000 men to put down the insurrection. He surrounded 200 Texans, including Davy Crockett and Jim Bowie, at the Alamo, an old abandoned mission. Refusing to surrender, the Texans held firm for ten days, but the Mexicans captured the Alamo and killed its defenders.

"REMEMBER THE ALAMO" became a rallying cry for the Texans who were steadfast in their quest for independence. Weeks later, while Santa Anna's troops took their afternoon siesta, Texans attacked. They were under the command of Sam Houston, who had fought against the Native Americans with Andrew Jackson in the War of 1812. By the end of the Battle of San Jacinto, the Texans captured Santa Anna, who promised, in exchange for his life, that he'd retreat from Texas. Thus, the Republic of Texas (nicknamed "the Lone Star Republic" because its flag bore a single star) received its independence.

IN THE MEXICAN-AMERICAN WAR'S AFTERMATH, Mexican-Americans lived as second-class citizens in territory they once owned. Many lost their land and livelihoods. In addition, the war reopened the sticky issue of slavery.

SAM HOUSTON IMMEDIATELY asked for Texas to be annexed to the United States, but as the balance of states stood at the time, there were thirteen states opposed to slavery and thirteen states in favor of it. Northerners felt that admitting Texas, where slavery was legal, would tip the balance of power in favor of the South. Thus, annexation was tabled until President John Tyler succeeded in pushing a joint resolution through Congress allowing Texas to join the Union in 1845.

★

WHEN ANNEXATION OCCURRED, Mexico severed all diplomatic ties to the United States. Mexicans were even more outraged when U.S. officials insisted that the Rio Grande be used as the southern border of Texas. Thus, border skirmishes ensued even as the new president, James Polk, offered to purchase California and New Mexico and to assume Mexico's debts in exchange for the Rio Grande border. When rumors of Mexican invasion caught the capital's attention, the president sent General Zachary Taylor and 3,500 troops to the Rio Grande to defend Texas. After Mexicans killed several of Taylor's men, Polk asked Congress to declare war, which it promptly did.

★

THE U.S. SOLDIERS who marched across the dry ground became covered with a white dust, similar in color and texture to Mexican adobes. Soon, Mexicans dubbed their opponents "dobies," or doughboys, and the name stuck for generations of soldiers.

★

IT DIDN'T TAKE long to capture California, and Americans also forced a Mexican surrender at Monterrey. President Polk then ordered troops south to capture Mexico City. Shortly thereafter, both sides reached peace.

PROTESTERS AGAINST THE Mexican War claimed it was immoral, proslavery, and against Republican values. Henry David Thoreau refused to pay his state (Massachusetts) taxes in protest and was placed in jail. Inspired by his arrest, Thoreau wrote "Civil Disobedience," which was studied by many, including Mahatma Gandhi and Martin Luther King.

AFTER TWO YEARS of fighting, the Treaty of Guadalupe Hidalgo resulted in Mexico's ceding California and large stretches of the Southwest to the United States, as well as its acceptance of the Rio Grande border. In return, the United States paid the Mexican government $15 million and assumed unpaid claims by U.S. citizens against Mexico. Zachary Taylor emerged as a hero and was elected president in 1848.

AFTER THE LOUISIANA PURCHASE spurred westward expansion in the early 1800s, the country experienced the continued growth of its boundaries. Many had the idea that the vast grasslands west of the Mississippi were unsuitable for farming, a theory that was promoted by explorers such as Lieutenant Zebulon Pike, an army officer who led a group from Saint Louis into Minnesota. Pike won command of a Southwest expedition that took him far into Spanish-held lands between 1806 and 1807.

IN WHAT IS now known as Colorado, the lieutenant discovered a mountain 14,110 feet (4,301 meters) high, now bearing the name Pikes Peak. Pike described much of the territory he discovered as a wasteland, and subsequent explorers concurred with the notion that the Great Plains region was bleak. Early settlers understandably avoided the plains.

IN 1818 AND 1842, treaties settled Canadian border disputes with Britain from northern Maine to the Continental Divide. England and America's disputed control of the Oregon Country was settled in 1846, with the United States gaining sovereignty of the region south of the 49th parallel. Now, the country spanned two oceans.

TIMBER HAS ALWAYS been a major export for Maine. During the Age of Sail (when people traveled mostly by sailing ships), Maine's tall white pine trees were used to make ships' masts, which hold up the sails. In fact, the very first sawmill in the United States was built in Maine, on the Piscataqua River in 1623.

DURING THE 1830s, Maine was the site of a border dispute between the United States and Canada. This conflict, called the Aroostook War, resulted in no deaths, and only a few bruises among the men who "fought" it. The long-term result of this so-called war was the Webster-Ashburton Treaty of 1842, which settled the boundary line between the United States and Canada not only in Maine, but along most of the rest of the border as well, making it the longest undefended international border in world history.

AROUND THIS TIME, members of a religious sect founded by Joseph Smith in 1830 sought isolation in the West, as they had been hounded in Ohio and Missouri, then Illinois and Iowa. Mormons, or members of the Church of Jesus Christ of Latter-day Saints, practiced polygamy and roused growing suspicion. In 1847, a group of Mormons ventured over the prairie through the Rocky Mountains until they reached the dreary flats beside the Great Salt Lake in Utah. Over the next several years, thousands followed the Mormon trail their leader had blazed. They called this homeland Zion, and like the Israelites of old, they made their desert bloom. By 1860, approximately 12,000 Mormons lived in the Salt Lake City environs.

ON JANUARY 24, 1848, just days before Mexico signed the treaty giving California to the United States, men working at a sawmill in the Sacramento Valley struck gold along the American River. Mill owner John Sutter implored his workers to keep the discovery quiet, but of course news spread, particularly from the lips of those who stood to profit. Samuel Brannan was one such shrewd merchant, who stocked his store near Sutter's fort with mining supplies before alerting others to the potential for riches.

THE GOLD STANDARD lasted until 1971 when President Nixon announced that the United States would no longer exchange dollars for gold. Now the United States is on a system of fiat money, which is used only as a medium of exchange.

IT TOOK ABOUT six months for news of the gold discovery to make it back East, but when it did, President Polk included word in his message to Congress. Thousands rushed west over the Great Plains, or by using the Oregon or Mormon Trails. Some took the Santa Fe, Sonora, or other southern trails, and still others went by boat to Panama and across to the city of Panama in order to catch another boat headed for San Francisco. Although it was a much longer voyage, some made their passage by sailing around Cape Horn, the southernmost point of South America—the demand was that great.

ALTHOUGH IT BEGAN in the spring of 1848, the gold rush grew slowly at first. It wasn't until 1849 that the largest numbers (tens of thousands) of people flooded across the continent and from all around the globe to converge on the area that would become California. Thus, those in hot pursuit of the precious metal became known as "forty-niners."

OF THOSE WHO trekked west, few struck it rich, but many stayed on to establish themselves in farming or business, increasing California's population nearly tenfold between 1848 and 1853. In 1850, California was admitted as a state. Gold rushes took place in the present-day states of Colorado, Nevada, Montana, Arizona, New Mexico, Idaho, Oregon, and Alaska.

WHEREVER A GOLD strike was made, miners gathered to build a camp or community that usually had a saloon and a gambling house, and very few women or children. Miners lived in shanties (hastily built wood-frame structures) that they could easily abandon when the gold ran out and everyone pulled up stakes to head for the next strike. Frontier justice reigned, and each camp set forth its own rules on the size of the gold claim that an individual could possess, and the way it should be registered. Sheriffs administered the codes, and justice was harsh and swift when necessary.

BY 1851 INDUSTRIAL mining became the trend where organized businesses with more advanced technology replaced individual efforts, and by the late 1850s, the California gold rush was over. Four decades later, others, in spite of the biting wind and frigid cold, trekked to Alaska when rich strikes were made near Nome and Fairbanks.

MOST IMMIGRANTS IN the 1800s came because of economic deprivation in their home countries, and African Americans came involuntarily from Africa as forced laborers to Southern plantation owners. New immigrants typically worked in menial, labor-intensive, low-paying, and dangerous jobs that the average American would shun. Because they were social outcasts until they assimilated into American society, immigrants usually stuck to themselves, maintaining their own cultural traditions and religions.

THE INFLUX OF so many immigrants, especially once they began intermarrying, brought about the phrase "melting pot," meaning that many immigrant traditions and bloodlines were blended together, creating a new society. Alarmed, Americans began to limit the numbers of immigrants as early as 1790, when Congress passed an act requiring a two-year residency period before one could qualify for U.S. citizenship. In 1795, that residency period rose to five years, and in 1798 during John Adams's administration, Congress passed the Alien and Sedition Acts.

THE NATURALIZATION ACT increased the waiting period to fourteen years, while the Alien Act allowed foreigners to be expelled if they were thought to threaten American interests. These acts were either repealed or expired in the early 1800s, but their passage was historic.

NO DOUBT THE greatest wave of immigrants to U.S. soil occurred between 1840 and the 1920s. During this period approximately 37 million immigrants arrived, mostly of German, Irish, Italian, English, Scottish, Austro-Hungarian, Scandinavian, Russian, Baltic, and Jewish descent.

THE INDUSTRIAL REVOLUTION, which began in England in the late eighteenth century and spread across Europe, changed the economic and social realities for many families, as did the potato famine that ravaged Ireland in the 1840s. Immigrants facing poverty at home believed American streets were paved with gold. Coming across in ships' steerage, many were swiftly disillusioned.

ABOUT 70 PERCENT of all European immigrants initially landed in New York City. If they came after 1892, most went through their processing and questioning at Ellis Island, which was opened after immigrants inundated Castle Garden on Manhattan Island. Some groups preferred to stay in New York City, while others made homes in Boston, Philadelphia, Baltimore, and New Orleans.

ELLIS ISLAND WAS an immigration station for about fifty years, from the 1890s until it closed in 1943. A little less than half of Americans (40 percent) had an ancestor pass through Ellis Island.

CHINESE IMMIGRANTS DURING THE 1850s entered through San Francisco and stayed in the region. But with railroads contributing to a transient society, many immigrants settled wherever they could find work. Those seeking heavy industry often moved inland to Buffalo, Pittsburgh, Cleveland, Detroit, Chicago, and Minneapolis. German immigrants settled extensively in Texas, the Midwest, New York, and Pennsylvania, where plenty of work was available in skilled labor or agriculture.

WHILE ITALIAN AMERICANS worked in light manufacturing, retail business, or the construction industry, Jewish Americans preferred to settle in major cities such as New York, Chicago, or Boston. Members of Slavic groups (Polish or Slovak Americans) found work in heavy manufacturing towns.

IN 1882, CONGRESS passed the Chinese Exclusion Act, which prevented Chinese immigration for ten years. This stemmed from economic hardship during the Arthur administration where Chinese and Irish immigrants vied for the few available jobs, and the tensions led to street fighting in San Francisco.

WOMEN IMMIGRANTS WORKED in laundries, retail shops, or light manufacturing; some, such as Irish American women, were employed as domestic servants.

IT OFTEN TOOK two or three generations for immigrants to move up the socioeconomic ladder and earn wages that could provide the comfortable standard of living that other Americans enjoyed.

A
SHATTERED
UNION

By the mid-1800s *there were many differences dividing the Northern and Southern states. The major difference lingered from the signing of the Constitution, when some statesmen opposed slavery while others clearly favored it. Slavery wasn't the only issue that divided the country, however. In the North, agricultural, commercial, and industrial development led to fast-growing cities, whereas in the South, the economy was dependent on foreign sales of cotton. In addition, the South opposed tariffs on imported goods, but the North's manufacturing economy demanded tariffs to stave off foreign competition. While you've probably read all about the issue of slavery and Abraham Lincoln's assassination, you'll find plenty of facts inside this chapter that you may not know about the growing tension between the North and the South during the 1800s.*

WHEN SLAVEHOLDING MISSOURI applied for statehood in 1818, there was a balance of slave states and free states, with eleven of each. Each faction viewed any attempt by the other faction to tip the scales as dangerous. Such fears delayed the annexation of Texas. Thus, Congress found a middle ground with what became known as the Missouri Compromise, enacted in 1820, which regulated the extension of slavery in the country for three decades until its repeal, in part, by the Kansas-Nebraska Act of 1854.

———————— ★ ————————

IN 1857, THE U.S. Supreme Court decided the case of Dred Scott, a fugitive slave who argued for his freedom after his master died when the two traveled to another state. When the Missouri state court ruled against Scott, he took his case to the Supreme Court, where Chief Justice Roger B. Taney had the final word, denying him the right to sue for his freedom, reasoning that a slave wasn't a citizen.

———————— ★ ————————

THE KANSAS-NEBRASKA ACT authorized the creation of Kansas and Nebraska, territories west and north of Missouri, and stipulated that the inhabitants of these territories would decide the legality of slavery. The bill's sponsor, Democratic senator Stephen A. Douglas of Illinois, wanted to assure Southern support for white settlement into otherwise Native American territory. He hoped such settlement would facilitate construction of the transcontinental railroad.

———————— ★ ————————

TENSIONS BETWEEN THE North and South grew more passionate after the Kansas-Nebraska Act. The vicious fighting that resulted became known as "Bleeding Kansas," and one of the names made famous over this dispute was John Brown, a self-ordained preacher with fervor against slavery. In May 1856, John Brown and his sons murdered five slave-supporting settlers in cold blood at Pottawatomic Creek.

THE ISSUE OF SLAVERY and the political fallout split the Democratic Party and destroyed the badly divided Whig Party, particularly in the South. The northern Whigs joined antislavery sentiment, forming the Republican Party in 1854.

THE COTTON GIN might even be blamed for the North-South turmoil. Invented by twenty-seven-year-old Eli Whitney in 1793, it made cleaning cottonseeds fifty times faster than by hand.

THERE WERE MANY advances in farming during this time. As far back as 1797, Charles Newbold, a New Jersey blacksmith, introduced the cast-iron moldboard plow. John Deere, another blacksmith, improved this plow in the 1830s, manufacturing it in steel. In 1831, twenty-two-year-old Cyrus McCormick invented the reaper, a machine that in only a few hours could cut an amount of grain that had taken two or three men a day to scythe by hand. Numerous other horse-drawn threshers, grain and grass cutters, cultivators, and other equipment made farming easier. By the late 1800s, steam power frequently replaced animal power in drawing plows and operating farm machinery.

SINCE THE BIRTH of the republic, states were fearful of tyranny and slow to release any powers to the federal government. In fact, the principle of nullification (legal theory that a state can nullify any federal law it deems unconstitutional) was supported by many of the early founders, among them James Madison and Thomas Jefferson, who elaborated the compact theory in the Virginia and Kentucky Resolutions. The New England states nullified an unpopular embargo from 1809 to 1810, and years later, Georgia nullified federal laws relating to Native Americans.

———————— ★ ————————

THE COMPACT THEORY claimed the nation was formed through a compact by the states, so consequently the national government is a creation of the states. The states therefore should be the final judges of whether or not the government has overstepped its boundaries.

———————— ★ ————————

THE ANTISLAVERY FACTION, comprised mostly of Northerners, helped fugitive slaves reach safety in a loose, secret network dubbed "the Underground Railroad," sometimes called "the Liberty Line." This enabled runaway slaves to achieve safety in the free states or in Canada. Of course, even in free states runaway slaves would not be safe, as the federal Fugitive Slave Law under the Compromise of 1850 required that they be returned to their owners.

———————— ★ ————————

BEGUN IN THE 1780s BY QUAKERS, the Underground Railroad is thought to have helped approximately 60,000 slaves gain freedom through its lifeline.

———————— ★ ————————

MANY HIDING OUT in the Underground Railroad traveled less conspicuously at night, using the North Star for guidance. Isolated farms or towns sympathetic to a slave's plight would effectively conceal them. Harriet Tubman, an escaped slave, became known as the Moses of the blacks for her work in rescuing slaves and leading them to freedom.

———————— ★ ————————

THE FEDERAL FUGITIVE SLAVE LAWS OF 1793 AND 1850 became difficult to enforce as Northern judges restricted the rights of many a slave's master in free states. This further enraged the Southern states, galvanizing sentiment toward Civil War.

———————— ★ ————————

ABRAHAM LINCOLN WAS born on February 12, 1809, in a log cabin that his father built in Kentucky. Because land titles were disputed in Kentucky, Abe's father moved the family to Pigeon Creek, Indiana (near Gentryville today), where the federal government was selling land, and Abe learned to wield an ax. In later years, his campaign hearkened back to these "rail splitter" days to prove that Abe came from humble roots.

———————— ★ ————————

LINCOLN WAS THE first president to be born outside of the original thirteen states of the Union. Other presidents, such as Jackson, Polk, Harrison, and Taylor, had moved to the frontier to make their fortunes, but all of the previous presidents had been born east of the Appalachian Mountains until Lincoln.

———————— ★ ————————

FROM BACKWOODS ORIGINS, Abraham Lincoln held many jobs in his lifetime—rail splitter, ferryboat captain, store clerk, surveyor, and postmaster among them. But the job that solidified his place as a great figure in history was his role as the sixteenth president of the United States during a time of great strife.

THE PRACTICE OF supporting the projects of other legislators in return for their support became known as *logrolling*, a term derived from a game of skill, especially among lumberjacks, in which two competitors try to balance on a floating log while spinning it with their feet.

IN THE SPRING of 1832, Lincoln decided to run for a seat in the Illinois House of Representatives. Before the election, he volunteered in the suppression of a rebellion by Native Americans led by Chief Black Hawk, though he saw no actual fighting. Despite a platform of better schools, roads, and canals, Lincoln was defeated, and he began a venture with a general store, followed by his job as a postmaster, a position that gave him ample time to read ravenously, especially newspapers.

LINCOLN RAN FOR the Illinois legislature again in 1834. He was elected every two years, and he studied law between legislative sessions. This experience as a state legislator sharpened his political savvy. Lincoln's first public stand on slavery, which he'd encountered years earlier when he viewed a slave auction, came in 1837 when the Illinois legislature voted to condemn abolition societies that wanted to end the practice by any means. Although Lincoln was opposed to slavery, he also felt strongly that extreme measures were not necessary and that lawful conduct could end the practice.

THOUGH LINCOLN BECAME a licensed lawyer in 1836 and continued as a state legislator, economic achievement didn't automatically follow and neither did success in a romantic relationship. He had lost his love, Ann Rutledge, and some time after her death he proposed marriage to another woman, who turned him down. It wasn't until he met Mary Todd in 1840 that courtship blossomed, and the two were married two years later.

ABRAHAM AND MARY TODD LINCOLN had four children, but only their eldest son, Robert Todd Lincoln, would survive to adulthood. It's said that Mary Todd Lincoln made her husband's life miserable, for she was unable to handle the loss of their children in later years. Though she was perhaps unstable, Lincoln remained devoted to her, and she in turn supported his political rise.

LINCOLN LOVED HIS high-strung wife, Mary, but there were times when he didn't pay attention to her. She would frequently make him pay for it. Once when she asked him to put a log on the fire when she was busy attending to their young children, Lincoln was so involved in a book he was reading that he didn't hear her and let the fire go out. Mary was so frustrated by this that she hit him in the head with a piece of firewood!

THE AMBITIOUS LEGISLATOR and lawyer soon looked beyond Illinois to the U.S. Congress, and he was elected in 1846 to the House of Representatives.

ILLINOIS CONSTITUENTS DENOUNCED him as a traitor when he opposed the Mexican-American War begun by President Polk, and in 1847, he called on Polk for proof of the president's insistence that the war began when Mexicans shed American blood on American soil. Once war was declared, however, Lincoln supported all appropriations, despite his private opinions.

———————— ★ ————————

ABOLITIONIST JOHN BROWN grew so obsessed with winning freedom for slaves that on October 16, 1859, he and approximately twenty others incited an uprising. Federal troops commanded by Robert E. Lee retaliated, killing about half the group, wounding Brown, and taking him prisoner. Brown was brought to trial and convicted of treason, murder, and criminal conspiracy. He was hanged on December 2, 1859.

———————— ★ ————————

BY 1856, THE Whig Party that Lincoln belonged to had died out, and the young politician officially identified himself as a Republican. As Senator Stephen Douglas ran for re-election, the Republicans nominated Abraham Lincoln to oppose him. Lincoln accepted the nomination.

———————— ★ ————————

ALTHOUGH LINCOLN LOST, the debates had more impact than the defeated candidate would imagine. They launched Lincoln onto the national stage, giving him opportunities to speak in other states. He spoke out against the extreme abolitionist John Brown, who incited violence. After speaking in New York, Lincoln became the leading contender for the Republican presidential nomination in 1860.

———————— ★ ————————

WHEN THE PARTY CONVENED, they did in fact select Lincoln as their presidential nominee. Though he won only 40 percent of the popular vote, he received the majority of electoral votes (though none in the South) and won the race to become the sixteenth president of the United States.

THE HOMESTEAD ACT OF 1862 gave settlers 160 acres of federal land for a nominal filing fee if they would farm it for five years. This federally owned land included property in all states except the original thirteen and Maine, Vermont, West Virginia, Kentucky, Tennessee, and Texas.

SOUTHERN MILITANTS HAD already threatened to secede from the Union if Lincoln was elected president. Sure enough, when election results became known, South Carolina became the first Southern state to leave the Union in December 1860. By February, several other states followed as they developed their own government.

BECAUSE RUMORS OF a possible assassination plot were rampant, Lincoln quietly sneaked into Washington at night for his inauguration on March 4, 1861. Ironically, Lincoln was sworn in as president by Chief Justice Roger B. Taney, who also issued the Dred Scott decision—a deed that spurred the crisis that would consume Lincoln's presidency.

FOLLOWING SOUTH CAROLINA'S SECESSION, Mississippi, Florida, Alabama, Georgia, Louisiana, and Texas adopted similar ordinances. The seceding states sent representatives to a convention in Montgomery, Alabama, where they adopted a provisional constitution, gave themselves a name, and chose a president of their own. Jefferson Davis of Mississippi was named president of the Confederacy, and the delegates ratified their separate constitution. Thus, the Confederate States of America (known as the Confederacy) was born.

———————— ★ ————————

MOST PEOPLE THINK of Richmond, Virginia, as the original capital of the Confederate States of America, but Virginia did not secede from the Union until many months after the states of the Deep South did. The capital was originally located in Montgomery, Alabama.

———————— ★ ————————

JEFFERSON DAVIS WAS born on June 3, 1808, in Kentucky. He was educated at Transylvania University in Lexington, Kentucky, and at the U.S. Military Academy. He served on the frontier following graduation until his health forced him to leave the army in 1835. From then on, Davis was a planter in Mississippi until he was elected to the U.S. Congress in 1845. When the Mexican War broke out a year later, he resigned his seat to serve, fighting at Monterrey and Buena Vista.

———————— ★ ————————

FOLLOWING THE WAR, Davis served as a U.S. senator from Mississippi, as secretary of war for President Franklin Pierce, and again as U.S. senator from 1857 to 1861. His legislative voice was heard arguing in support of states' rights, and he used his influence during the Pierce administration to pass the Kansas–Nebraska Act, favoring a proslavery sentiment. Ironically,

Davis didn't favor secession. As a senator, he tried to keep the Southern states in the Union, although when his own state of Mississippi seceded, he gave up his Senate seat.

———————— ★ ————————

FRANKLIN PIERCE HAD to convince Jefferson Davis (whom he knew from both the U.S. Senate and the army during the Mexican War) to serve as his secretary of war. Davis was a talented administrator and reformed the army, making it more efficient and better at doing its job. Here's the strange part: Within four years Davis would be trying to defeat the army he had reorganized and rebuilt once he was elected president of the Confederate States of America.

———————— ★ ————————

JAMES BUCHANAN, who succeeded Pierce as our 15th president, fell in love and became engaged to a girl named Anne Coleman in 1819. At one point the couple argued, and Anne broke off the engagement. While away visiting relatives, she died suddenly, apparently of suicide. Buchanan was devastated. He swore he would never marry, and he never did. He was our only bachelor president. His niece (who was an orphan at a young age but Buchanan raised her from childhood) performed the duties of the first lady during his administration.

———————— ★ ————————

ON MAY 24, 1861, the Confederates moved their capital from Montgomery, Alabama, to Richmond, Virginia. When created, the Confederacy had a population of almost 9 million, including nearly 4 million slaves. But that paled by comparison to the Union population of approximately 22 million. Land values were higher in the North, as was economic strength, making the South extremely dependent on Europe for many material items.

———————— ★ ————————

DAVIS DID APPOINT General Robert E. Lee as commander of the Army of Northern Virginia, and Davis remained true to his task until the bitter end. He staunchly believed the South could achieve independence, until he realized that defeat was imminent. He fled the Confederate capital of Richmond, and on May 10, 1865, federal troops captured him in Georgia. For two years he was imprisoned at Fortress Monroe in Virginia. He was indicted for treason, but released one year later on bond.

——————— ★ ———————

FORT SUMTER, which lay at the entrance to the Charleston harbor, remained under the command of Major Robert Anderson and a small detachment of federal troops. It was by far the most important of the four forts remaining under Union control after Lincoln's election.

——————— ★ ———————

HARRIET BEECHER STOWE was an American writer and abolitionist who wrote a powerful novel—*Uncle Tom's Cabin*—that precipitated the Civil War as it strengthened the antislavery movement. Legend has it that when President Lincoln met Harriet Beecher Stowe, he said, "So you're the little lady who started the Civil War."

——————— ★ ———————

RELUCTANTLY, BECAUSE HE feared igniting war, President Lincoln sent supplies to reinforce Fort Sumter, but the Confederates blocked the harbor. With orders from President Jefferson Davis of the Confederacy, General Beauregard demanded that the Union surrender the fort. When Major Anderson ignored the ultimatum, Confederate fire erupted on April 12, 1861, and Anderson had little choice but to surrender.

——————— ★ ———————

EVEN IN 2000, South Carolina's allegiance to its Confederate past was strong. Angry protests surrounded the flying of the Confederate battle flag over South Carolina's statehouse dome between 1962 and 2000. On July 1, 2000, the flag was moved from the dome to another location on the statehouse lawn.

EARLY IN THE CIVIL WAR, Lincoln removed Brigadier General Irvin McDowell from his command of the federal army and placed Major General George B. McClellan in the role. While McClellan restored morale and raised the caliber of the fighting forces, he lacked decisiveness and was very slow.

UNION SOLDIERS DRESSED in blue government-issued uniforms, whereas the South's official color was gray. However, as some clothing worn by Confederate soldiers came from Union casualties or their own clothing reserves, the dress code varied a bit.

IN JULY 1861, at the Battle of Bull Run, or what the South called First Manassas, the Confederates used some of the brightest and best in military talent to defeat the rather haphazard Union soldiers marching into Virginia. The Confederate army of General Beauregard maintained a line along Bull Run Creek (or Manassas Junction), and the Virginia brigade led by Thomas J. Jackson was at the line's center. His stubborn defense earned him the nickname "Stonewall Jackson," for his troops remained standing like a stone wall.

IN FEBRUARY 1862, Union gunboats led by Commodore Andrew Foote steamed up the Tennessee River to reach Fort Henry, where the plan called for an amphibious attack en route to Fort Donelson on the Cumberland River. Ulysses S. Grant led forces on land, but the muddy roads they traversed slowed them. Foote grew impatient and fired, wrecking havoc with the fort's walls and Rebel guns. With floodwaters flowing in, the Southern forces raised the white flag.

———————— ★ ————————

AFTER GRANT ALLOWED his name change to Ulysses S. Grant, he began to be called by a number of nicknames arising from it. First, because he was now U.S. Grant, his compatriots in the army called him "Uncle Sam," eventually shortening it to just "Sam." Later, when he was a successful battlefield general during the Civil War, Grant earned the nickname "Unconditional Surrender."

———————— ★ ————————

MOST OF THE escaping Confederates sought shelter at Fort Donelson. Grant's army pursued them by land, reinforced by the gunboats making their way up the river. But with this fort situated high on a bluff, the fire by water did little but cause a retaliatory hail of bullets. Union soldiers broke Confederate lines and caused acting General Buckner to surrender. Buckner, who had known Grant before the Civil War, expected generous surrender terms. That was wishful thinking, for Grant demanded unconditional and immediate surrender, earning him the nickname "Unconditional Surrender" Grant. Soon after these forts were taken, Union troops took Tennessee's capital at Nashville, giving them a commanding presence in Southern territory, especially along the rivers. The march farther south commenced.

———————— ★ ————————

MORE THAN 150 prisons were established during the Civil War. All were filled beyond capacity, with inmates crowded into camps and shelters with meager provisions. Although precise figures may never be known, an estimated 56,000 men perished in Civil War prisons, a casualty rate far greater than any battle during the war.

IN EARLY APRIL 1862, Grant was in a holding pattern in Tennessee while he waited for another Union commander to join him in a campaign toward Corinth, Mississippi. However, Confederate commander Albert Johnston's troops struck Grant's army by surprise. Grant lost approximately 13,000 men and the Confederates almost as many in a bloody battle known as Shiloh (ironically, the Hebrew word for "place of peace").

WITH GENERAL MCCLELLAN in charge, the Union army began its Peninsular campaign, advancing by way of the peninsula between the James and York Rivers in Virginia in order to reach Richmond, the Confederate capital. But McClellan was not a decisive leader, and he was dreadfully slow, delaying the assault on Richmond. The resulting Seven Days Battle, fought in late June 1862, led to an alarming number of casualties. Lincoln's administration held McClellan responsible for not taking Richmond, while McClellan blamed the president for not sending reinforcements.

THOUGH MOST OF the nation's attention was focused on the peninsula, the Union needed to gain control of New Orleans if it ever wanted to navigate the Mississippi River and effectively blockade the South. In April 1862, Flag Officer David Farragut, with a squadron of ships carrying federal troops, started up the Mississippi and arrived on April 25, demanding surrender. As the Confederates numbered only 3,000, they gave up easily, inflicting a painful loss on the South.

———————— ★ ————————

UPON THE FAILURE of the Peninsular campaign, Lincoln named Henry Halleck as the top general of the Union armies. Halleck ordered McClellan to bring his men back to Washington, for Lincoln was not about to leave Washington, DC, unguarded. Organized in June 1862, the Army of Virginia had 45,000 troops and a fresh commander, Major General John Pope. Pope soon marched south with hopes of taking Richmond.

———————— ★ ————————

WITH OTHERS IN HIS COMPANY, Lee rushed to join Jackson, and on August 25, 1862, Confederate forces moved in on the Union at Manassas, capturing their supply station and treating themselves to a feast of food. On August 29, Pope's men attacked Jackson's soldiers. The Confederate defensive was weak, and Pope fully believed he'd defeated Jackson. He even wired Washington of his victory. Then on the following day, the Confederates reinforced Jackson, defeating the Union's forces. This battle became known as the Second Battle of Bull Run.

———————— ★ ————————

WHEN MCCLELLAN CONTINUED to be a hesitant leader, Lincoln replaced him with Major General Ambrose Burnside. But in December 1862, Lee defeated Burnside at Fredericksburg, Virginia, south of the Rappahannock River, in a long day of needless slaughter. Refusing to heed the warnings of fellow generals, Burnside sent his troops into Lee's fire.

———————— ★ ————————

LINCOLN RELIEVED BURNSIDE of his command and put Major General Joseph Hooker in place. "Fighting Joe," as he was called, set off to outfox Lee in late April 1863. He jumped most of his troops upstream of Lee's forces on the Rappahannock, but Hooker must have gotten spooked, for he quickly ordered his men onto the defensive. Now Lee had the advantage and used it, striking hard. The fighting was so intense that fire erupted in the dry leaves and brush, choking the battle lines with smoke and burning some soldiers alive. Hooker pulled back his army across the Rappahannock, having lost 17,000 of his fighting force.

LINCOLN RELIEVED HOOKER and Pope of their command, giving McClellan, or "Little Mac," another chance to fend off Lee's troops. Luckily for McClellan, a Confederate soldier left behind a precious piece of military intelligence—General Lee's troop orders. But in another surprise, a Southern sympathizer tipped off General Lee that the North knew of his plans. As a result, Lee pulled back his forces, and instead of attacking quickly, the cautious-as-ever McClellan hesitated, believing that Lee outnumbered him. In the fighting that September 1862, McClellan drove Lee back into Virginia in the bloodiest one-day battle ever fought. The Battle of Antietam, or Sharpsburg as the South called it, cost both sides dearly, but the outcome was Union victory.

ON JULY 3, 1863, at 1 P.M., Confederates opened an artillery bombardment—with 175 cannons firing on the Union line—during the Battle of Gettysburg. General Pickett, with a fresh division, led a charge on Cemetery Ridge. The Union army fired on the Confederate troops, inflicting heavy casualties. The bloody charge failed to crack General Meade's line. The Confederates fell back, having lost nearly three-fourths of their ranks. Pickett's charge ensured that the Battle of Gettysburg was just about over. Indeed, on the evening of July 4, General Lee began retreating to Virginia.

BY SUMMER 1863, General Lee's army was at its fighting peak, anxious to threaten northern territory. Lee commanded his army through Gettysburg, Pennsylvania, in order to march further north. Lee tried to get General Richard Ewell to seize Cemetery Hill, just south of the town, but Ewell was too cautious, and the Union set up a line along the ridges during the night. Confederates did capture Devil's Den, a boulder-strewn area in front of the hill known as Little Round Top. Had they put cannons atop Little Round Top, they could have blasted the Union line. Once the Rebels were spotted, however, fighting recommenced, and Little Round Top was saved.

DURING AUGUST AND SEPTEMBER 1862, the Confederate army invaded Kentucky, a slave state that had not seceded from the Union. Kentuckians were divided, and it wasn't uncommon to have people from the same community enlist in both the Confederate and Union armies. They clashed at the Battle of Perryville on October 8, 1862. Neither side could claim victory, but the Confederates retreated.

GENERAL LONGSTREET OF the Confederacy had warned Lee not to attack the Union's center of the line. On the third day, in what became known as Pickett's Charge, Confederates opened a huge artillery bombardment concentrating on the line's center. This lapse in judgment forced Lee to retreat back across the Potomac. At Gettysburg the Union fielded 83,300 men and sustained 23,000 casualties. The Confederacy fielded 75,100 men and sustained 28,100 casualties.

LINCOLN WAS CALLED upon to deliver just a few appropriate remarks on November 19, 1863, to dedicate a military cemetery at Gettysburg. He delivered his remarks following those of Edward Everett, a distinguished speaker in his own right. Though Lincoln's speech was much more concise than the two-hour oration Everett rendered, the president's remarks were profound and masterful, imparting another persuasive vision for America.

---------- ★ ----------

THE GETTYSBURG ADDRESS was only 284 words long. Lincoln got up and gave the speech so quickly that the photographer assigned to cover the event didn't have enough time to change the film in his camera before Lincoln had sat down again.

---------- ★ ----------

ONE PERSISTENT MYTH is that Lincoln composed the speech while riding on the train from Washington to Gettysburg and wrote it on the back of an envelope or a napkin. This story is at odds with the existence of several early drafts and the reports of Lincoln's final editing while a guest of David Wills in Gettysburg.

---------- ★ ----------

LINCOLN, UNDER MUCH pressure from abolitionists, saw his main objective as saving the Union, regardless of how the slavery issue played out. With the political climate simply too volatile, Lincoln trod carefully so as not to offend slaveholding Border States, very key to the North. Kentucky was one of these. Because of its strategic location on the Ohio River, it had to remain in the Union. Besides, in his inaugural address, Lincoln had promised not to interfere with slavery. To do so would have meant additional states joining the Confederacy.

---------- ★ ----------

ON APRIL 16, 1862, Lincoln signed a bill abolishing slavery in Washington, DC. Lincoln wanted to free all the slaves in the seceding states, but Secretary of State William Seward advised him to make such a momentous announcement only after a Union victory. When the Battle of Antietam brought that opportunity, and as he became more confident of Border State support, Lincoln issued his Emancipation Proclamation. On September 22, 1862, he announced that on January 1, 1863, all slaves residing in the Confederate states would be free.

————— ★ —————

LINCOLN PUSHED FOR the Thirteenth Amendment, which made up for the limitations of the Emancipation Proclamation: it barred slavery from the United States in perpetuity. Later, it became a condition that Southern states had to accept the amendment to be readmitted to the Union. It became law in January 1865.

————— ★ —————

THE PROCLAMATION DIDN'T apply to the Border States, which were not in rebellion against the Union, though Lincoln did urge voluntary compensated emancipation. In fact, Lincoln did not have the power to free slaves except under the powers granted during war to seize enemy property. As president, he had to abide by the Constitution, which protected slavery in slave states. Due to their rebellion, he could act in states that had seceded. The 100-day warning in the proclamation was intended to give Rebel states ample opportunity to rejoin the Union with slavery intact.

————— ★ —————

WHEN ABRAHAM LINCOLN was working on drafts of his Emancipation Proclamation, he had the foresight to say, "If my name ever goes down into history, it will be for this act, and my whole soul is in it." Drafted in 1862, it went into effect by presidential signature on New Year's Day, 1863.

---- ★ ----

USUALLY, LINCOLN SIGNED bills in abbreviated form using "A. Lincoln." However, he signed his full signature onto the Emancipation Proclamation, and said to those cabinet officers standing near, "Gentlemen, I never, in my life, felt more certain that I was doing right than in signing this paper."

---- ★ ----

FURTHER ALONG IN his address, Lincoln invited slaves to join the Union army. By the end of the Civil War, one Union soldier in eight was African American. This hastened the South's demise, and foreign governments (namely France and Great Britain) took notice as well.

---- ★ ----

THE DRAFT (CONSCRIPTION) began in 1862 when the Confederacy called all men between eighteen and forty-five to serve in the army. In March 1863, the Union passed a similar act calling men between twenty and forty-five into military service. However, you could hire a substitute or pay $300 instead.

---- ★ ----

THE UNION FACED additional burdens with financing the war. As a result, new federal taxes were levied on inheritances, legal documents, and personal income. The government also printed paper money, dubbed "greenbacks" because of the color. By 1863, $450 million worth of greenbacks were in use. The value of these greenbacks varied and was usually lower than that of gold.

——————— ★ ———————

LINCOLN EASILY WON the 1864 election against Democratic candidate General McClellan. McClellan's followers felt Lincoln unjustly relieved him of his military command following Antietam. Showing himself to be a staunch fighter, McClellan ignored his party's platform, which called for the war's immediate end. Instead, he urged that the fighting continue. Lincoln chose Andrew Johnson as his vice president and ran on the platform of abolishing slavery and ending the war.

——————— ★ ———————

ON THE DAY Lee withdrew his forces from Gettysburg, Lincoln received word that General Ulysses S. Grant had captured Vicksburg, Mississippi, a key Confederate fort along the Mississippi River. Indeed the Battle of Vicksburg had spilled over from October 1862 until July of 1863. With no relief army in sight, the Confederates had asked Grant for surrender terms, and on July 4, 1863, the Rebels stacked their arms before marching out of their fallen city. Grant's victory opened the Mississippi River to the Union and effectively broke the Confederate army in two.

——————— ★ ———————

BY THE END OF 1863, the Union had achieved two main objectives—control of the Mississippi River, which split the South in two, and a strangling blockade of Southern ports. Severely lacking, however, was a coordinated strategy to finish the war, until in March 1864, Lincoln selected General Ulysses S. Grant to command the Northern troops.

GENERAL GRANT GAVE General William Tecumseh Sherman full command of the West, while he himself moved east to lead Meade's Army of the Potomac against General Lee's Confederate forces. His strategy: attack the South's strong armies rather than take key Southern cities. While Grant would focus on Lee, Sherman's march through Georgia went after General Joe Johnston's force of 45,000 men. While en route, he hoped to destroy much of the Confederate infrastructure, especially the vital rail and industrial strength of Atlanta.

ON SEPTEMBER 1, 1864, Sherman succeeded in his mission, sending a telegram to the president that "Atlanta is ours." The capture did much to solidify Lincoln's re-election.

LEE'S ARMY OF Northern Virginia spent much of the fall and winter of 1864–65 hunkered down in trenches. In March 1865, he decided to attack the Union's Fort Stedman long enough to divert Grant and, he hoped, effect an escape to join Joseph E. Johnston's forces farther south. But the attempt failed, and Lee took his dwindling troops toward Lynchburg. The Rebel lines collapsed at Sailor's Creek, and finally, desertion, disease, near-starvation, and the Union's relentless attacks brought the Confederacy to its knees.

IN A QUIET country village near a rail stop, General Robert E. Lee brought his weary regiments into the Appomattox Courthouse. Calling a truce, Lee asked for a meeting with Grant to discuss surrender terms. On the afternoon of April 9, 1865, the two generals met at the home of Virginian Wilmer McLean. While they chatted about the Mexican War initially, Grant knew that whatever they discussed regarding the Civil War's end would have a profound effect on the country's restoration.

IN HIS OFFER TO LEE, Grant stated that Confederate forces could keep their own horses, baggage, and sidearms, returning home with the assurance that U.S. authorities would not harm them. Grant even made arrangements to feed Lee's troops before the two parted.

Lee's army stacked its arms and surrendered battle flags on April 12, 1865, though it took until June for all Confederate forces to lay down their arms.

THE SENATE AND House passed the Thirteenth Amendment, eliminating slavery in 1864 and 1865, respectively, while the country was still waging war. Those states that had seceded had to approve of the amendment in order to be readmitted to the Union.

AFTER THE WAR, the Republican majority in Congress pushed through the Fourteenth Amendment, which defined American citizenship to include all former slaves and declared that individual states could not unlawfully deny citizens their rights and privileges. Just like the amendment that had preceded it, seceding states had to adopt the Fourteenth Amendment to be readmitted. The required three-fourths of the states ratified the Fourteenth Amendment on July 9, 1868, though the measure had passed Congress two years earlier.

THE FIFTEENTH AMENDMENT, granting African American men the right to vote, also took a two-year path to ratification. It was presented to the states in 1868, and Southern states grudgingly passed the measure. Years later (in the 1890s), former Confederate states required African Americans to take literacy tests as a requirement for voting. Since few slaves were literate at the time, this all but eliminated voting among this group until a more modern civil rights movement protested these strictures in subsequent years.

THE CIVIL WAR took more than 600,000 lives, destroyed property valued at $5 billion, and created social wounds that never completely healed. It did, however, end slavery, making many believe the moral objectives of the war were indeed accomplished.

ON GOOD FRIDAY, APRIL 14, 1865, Lincoln and his wife, along with General and Mrs. Grant, were to attend a performance of *Our American Cousin* at Ford's Theatre in Washington, DC. Although the Grants could not attend, the Lincolns went to the theater with their other guests. At approximately 10:30 P.M. and at a planned moment when all eyes were focused on the stage, John Wilkes Booth, a Southern sympathizer, crept into the poorly protected presidential box and fired his pistol at Lincoln's head just once.

LINCOLN'S BODY WAS taken to a lodging house across the street, where Mrs. Lincoln, cabinet members, and friends waited through the night for doctors to perform a miracle that never happened. On Saturday, April 15, 1865, Lincoln was pronounced dead, and within hours, Vice President Andrew Johnson was sworn in as president. This marked the first presidential assassination in the United States.

LINCOLN'S BODY LAY in state in the East Room of the White House. On April 19, he was given a military funeral in Washington, and two days later, his coffin was placed on a special train that carried his body back to Springfield, Illinois, for burial in Oak Ridge Cemetery. The slain president's funeral procession retraced the route he'd initially taken to reach Washington for his inauguration in 1861.

JOHN WILKES BOOTH was a vengeful, half-crazed actor from a fairly famous theatrical family who had planned for some time to kidnap the president and take him to Richmond. There, he hoped to exchange him for captured Confederate prisoners of war. However, when that city fell and with the conflict now resolved, Booth resorted to murder, claiming that he was God's instrument to punish Lincoln for all the trouble he had caused the country.

ON THE SAME day that Booth shot Lincoln, friends of Booth made attempts on Secretary Seward's life, but he lived. In fact, one friend was to have carried out a plan to assassinate Vice President Johnson, but decided against it.

BOOTH ESCAPED WITH the help of friends and an unsuspecting physician who tended his injuries, but he was discovered twelve days later in a shack near Bowling Green, Virginia. When he refused to surrender to authorities, they set the barn ablaze. Some say that Booth was struck by a sniper's shot, and others assert that he pulled a gun on himself. Regardless, Booth was dragged out of the inferno and died shortly thereafter. His coconspirators went on trial for aiding the assassin. They were tried, and convicted, by a military tribunal rather than a civil court.

★

MARY ELIZABETH JENKINS SURRATT was an American boarding house owner who was convicted of taking part in the conspiracy to assassinate President Abraham Lincoln. She was the first woman in the United States to be executed.

MENDING
THE NATION

At the start of the Civil War, Andrew Johnson, a Tennessee Democrat, was the only Southern U.S. senator remaining loyal to the Union. You can imagine this didn't win him many friends, even if it did earn him the vice-presidential nomination in the 1864 election. Thrust into the presidency after a mere forty-one days on the job as second in command, Johnson tried to reunite the bitterly divided land that saw neighbor fight against neighbor, brother against brother. Rebuilding the nation after such a harsh and bitter divide was no easy feat, and inside this chapter, you'll learn about all the people and movements that helped get the nation reunited again.

PRESIDENT ANDREW JOHNSON never stopped making and mending his own clothes. He sewed most of his own clothes during his presidency, and did the same for many of the members of his cabinet.

JOHNSON SHARED LINCOLN'S view favoring leniency toward the Southern states, but a group of congressmen called the Radical Republicans resented Johnson's Reconstruction policies. Reconstruction was the official name given the rebuilding process following the American Civil War. It forced the country to grapple with pressing questions that came up after Southern defeat and the abolition of slavery, like whether there should be punishment for the Confederate rebellion and what rights would be granted to the newly freed slaves.

JOHNSON'S SECRETARY OF STATE, William H. Seward, acquired land that would become Alaska from Russia. Critics called him mad to pay $7.2 million for unexplored territory to the north. Seward reached the deal in 1867, and it was quickly ridiculed as "Seward's Folly." It wasn't until the Alaskan gold rush years later that Seward's shrewd purchase would be appreciated.

JOHNSON OFFERED AMNESTY to all who took the oath of allegiance (and if the Confederates had postwar wealth surpassing $20,000, they had to apply for a pardon). He returned plantations to their former owners, and he sought to restore political rights to the Southern states as soon as possible, with each state drafting a new constitution. Of course, these constitutions had to outlaw slavery and disavow secession.

THE FACTION AGAINST President Johnson grew in its belief that the Union victory had to stand for more than simple restoration. The Republican majority in the House of Representatives refused to seat their colleagues sent by Southern states or to accept the legitimacy of their governments.

— ★ —

CONGRESS PASSED ITS version of the Reconstruction Act in March 1867 over Johnson's veto. Some Southern states were given a military commander to oversee the writing of new state constitutions that would allow all adult males to vote, regardless of race. If states ratified their new constitutions along with the Fourteenth Amendment, they would be readmitted to the Union.

— ★ —

IN 1868, ANDREW JOHNSON became the first president to be put on trial by the Senate, even though no constitutional grounds existed for his impeachment. Johnson was spared from removal by a margin of one vote. But his presidency was effectively over, based on the political disagreements stemming from his Reconstruction policies.

— ★ —

WHILE THE U.S. WAR DEPARTMENT created the Freedmen's Bureau in 1865 to help former slaves find jobs and obtain an education, Southern whites did what they could to keep African Americans poor and powerless.

— ★ —

CONFEDERATE WAR VETERANS formed the Ku Klux Klan, originally a social organization, which quickly became a violent vigilante group preventing freedmen from voting. This hate group originated in Pulaski, Tennessee, with its members, often dressed in white robes with pointed hoods, spreading terror as they rode on horseback at night.

RADICAL REPUBLICANS IN CONGRESS such as Benjamin Butler urged President Ulysses S. Grant to take action against the Ku Klux Klan. Congress passed the Ku Klux Act and it became law in 1871. This gave the president the power to intervene in troubled states. Shortly thereafter, the organization practically disappeared. The founding of the second Ku Klux Klan in 1915 was inspired by, among other things, an anti-immigrant and anti-Semitic agenda and a glorified version of the original Klan presented in the film *The Birth of a Nation* in 1915.

THOUGH TREATED AS second-class citizens, blacks eagerly sought to make a better life for themselves. Most blacks continued to vote Republican, but Democrats returned to power in some Southern states by the mid-1870s. Democratic victories sometimes led to a reversal of Reconstruction accomplishments, and over many decades to come, black school funding was slashed and a rigid segregation policy pervaded the South. As a result, Southern blacks began their migration north to escape the lingering oppression. Many settled in America's largest cities, such as New York and Chicago.

THE WILD WEST refers to a time and place in American history surrounding the settlement of the western states in the second half of the nineteenth century.

COWBOYS EPITOMIZED a unique type of Western character, and they figured prominently after the Civil War through the 1890s when transportation facilities were scanty. Cowboys had to drive cattle to shipping points over long distances, and they often had to keep the livestock safe from thieves and marauding animals. Because these hardy souls were tough at times, the cowboy figure reached mythical status, becoming legend.

ONE OF THE most colorful figures of the Old West was born William Frederick Cody in Iowa in 1846. He earned his nickname for his hunting skill while supplying Kansas Pacific Railroad workers with buffalo meat. His Buffalo Bill's Wild West show featured real cowboys and real Native Americans portraying the "real West." By the turn of the century, Buffalo Bill was one of the most famous and most recognizable men in the world.

PEOPLE SUCH AS the Earp brothers, led by the famous Wyatt Earp, went to the Old West looking to get rich quick. The Earps eventually got into a power struggle with another local family, the Clantons. This power struggle led to the most famous gunfight in western history: the gunfight at the OK Corral.

ON CHRISTMAS DAY, 1851, a spark from one of the building's chimneys set the Library of Congress on fire. Nearly two-thirds of the Library's collection of over 50,000 books was destroyed. When he heard about the blaze, President Fillmore himself went down to help fight the fire, carrying buckets for the brigade with his own two hands.

TOWNS SUCH AS Abilene, Kansas, prospered in the late 1860s and throughout the next decade as cattle were loaded and shipped by rail to eastern markets.

CHEYENNE, WYOMING, WAS founded and became prominent as a division point for the Union Pacific Railroad.

DODGE CITY, KANSAS, was founded in 1872 with the arrival of the railroad and developed into a major shipping point for trail herds.

IN 1868, CONGRESS had recognized the Black Hills of South Dakota as sacred to the Sioux and Cheyenne, but the deal was called off when gold was discovered there. It became common practice for the government to move Native Americans onto reservations whenever their current settlements impeded so-called progress.

ON JUNE 25, 1876, federal cavalry with George A. Custer in the lead attacked the camp of Chief Sitting Bull on the Little Big Horn River in Montana. The Native Americans prevailed, killing Custer and his troops, but their victory was short-lived. Federal troops later forced the Native Americans to surrender.

———— ★ ————

IN 1863, THE Nez Perce were ordered to a reservation following the discovery of gold on their lands. Chief Joseph the Elder denounced the United States, destroyed his American flag and his Bible, and refused to move his band from the Wallowa Valley or sign the treaty that would make the new reservation boundaries official. After his death in 1871, his son, Chief Joseph, continued the resistance of the Nez Perce to the resettlement orders of the federal government. After a 1,400-mile march toward Idaho and then Canada, Chief Joseph and his band of 700 finally surrendered to federal troops numbering more than 2,000.

★

ULYSSES S. GRANT, who became a national hero after leading the Union to victory in the Civil War, was inaugurated as president in 1869. He served two terms despite scandals within his administration involving railroad fraud and whiskey taxes.

★

RUTHERFORD B. HAYES succeeded Grant, winning a controversial election by one electoral vote over Samuel J. Tilden. As a result, he was sometimes referred to as "His Fraudulency" or "Rutherfraud" B. Hayes. Fairly lenient toward the South, Hayes won over his critics by the end of his single term in office.

★

NEITHER PRESIDENT HAYES nor his wife drank alcohol, and Hayes was the first president to ban alcohol in the White House, even during official state functions. His wife, Lucy, directed that lemonade be served during all official occasions, ceremonies, and state dinners. This practice earned her the nickname "Lemonade Lucy."

JAMES A. GARFIELD came to the presidency in 1881, making him the third Civil War general in a row to become president.

PRESIDENT GARFIELD WAS naturally left-handed and taught himself to write with both hands. When he was an adult, he loved to show off at parties by writing with his left hand in Greek and with his right hand in Latin, both at the same time!

GARFIELD WAS PROBABLY safer on the battlefield though, for tragedy struck four months into his presidency: he was shot by Charles Guiteau, a disgruntled man who had failed to obtain a federal job. Garfield survived with his gunshot injuries for two months, dying on September 19, 1881.

IN 1881, THE United States had three presidents within one year. President Rutherford B. Hayes had left office at the end of his term in March of that year, and President James A. Garfield had taken office that same month. When President Garfield died that same year, it became only the second time in American history that the United States had three presidents serving during the same year. The first time it happened was in 1841 when President Martin Van Buren had left office in March, followed by William Henry Harrison, who died after only a month as president and who was in turn succeeded by John Tyler. It has not happened since.

UPON GARFIELD'S DEATH, Chester A. Arthur was sworn in. Ironically, this man who had formerly been given political jobs in return for party loyalty became a staunch supporter of earning federal jobs based on merit. In 1883, Arthur signed the Pendleton Act, which established the Civil Service Commission, requiring job seekers to pass examinations before being admitted to civil service.

HAVING FAILED TO win the Republican Party's nomination for a second term, Arthur left office. Grover Cleveland then served two terms as president, though not consecutively. He was ousted from office by Benjamin Harrison in 1889, but returned to the White House four years later. Cleveland won the popular vote 49 to 48 percent, but Harrison triumphed in the Electoral College, becoming president.

GROVER CLEVELAND WAS the only president to be elected to two nonconsecutive terms of office in American history. Other presidents, such as Martin Van Buren and Millard Fillmore, were nominated for the presidency by small political parties long after they had left the White House, but only Cleveland has served two different terms as president of the United States.

IN HIS TWO terms, Cleveland earned the nickname of "Old Veto," for he vetoed more legislation than any prior president.

DURING A SEVERE economic depression, known as the Panic of 1893, Cleveland failed to restore the nation's sagging economy and didn't win a third nomination.

PRESIDENT BENJAMIN HARRISON, the 23rd president, came from a very distinguished political family. His great-grandfather, Benjamin Harrison, was a signer of the Declaration of Independence, his grandfather, William Henry Harrison, was the ninth president of the United States, and his father, John, was a U.S. congressman from Ohio.

HARRISON SUPPORTED the Sherman Antitrust Act of 1890 designed to regulate big business and eliminate monopolies. He also signed the McKinley Tariff Act, which placed tariffs on imported goods, causing a rise in prices.

THE ORIGINAL PLEDGE OF ALLEGIANCE was written by Christian Socialist Francis Bellamy in 1892. The phrase "my flag" was in the original. An act of Congress in 1954 inserted the words "under God" in part as a Cold War patriotic response to the Soviet Union's prohibitions on religion.

IN 1896, OHIO governor William McKinley needed someone from the East Coast to be his running mate for the presidential election of that year. Hobart, a career state legislator in the strategically important state of New Jersey, could help McKinley win that important state. McKinley won New Jersey in the election in part because of Hobart's name on the ticket. He served as vice president for two years, with his health declining for the last several months. Had he lived a couple more years, another political outsider named Theodore Roosevelt might never have been president.

WILLIAM MCKINLEY CAME to office in 1897 and quickly established his reputation in foreign affairs. In 1895, Cubans had risen up against their Spanish rulers, and in January 1898, McKinley ordered the U.S. battleship *Maine* to Havana harbor to check on the hostilities. One month later, the *Maine* exploded and sunk, killing 262 sailors. Having accused Spain of this deliberate attack, the United States declared war on April 25.

———————— ★ ————————

THEODORE ROOSEVELT, SECRETARY OF THE NAVY at the time of the attack on the U.S. battleship *Maine*, quit his post and formed a cavalry unit of volunteer soldiers. Known as the Rough Riders, these men landed in Cuba in June, heading inland toward San Juan Ridge. On horseback, armed with a pistol, Roosevelt led his men to victory.

———————— ★ ————————

THE SPANISH-AMERICAN WAR lasted 113 days, ending with the Treaty of Paris. Under the terms of the treaty, Spain left Cuba, giving Puerto Rico and Guam to the United States along with the Philippines, for which the United States paid $20 million.

———————— ★ ————————

DURING PRESIDENT MCKINLEY'S ADMINISTRATION, the nation annexed Hawaii as a territory.

———————— ★ ————————

ON SEPTEMBER 6, 1901, an anarchist from Buffalo, New York, shot President William McKinley. Eight days later, the president died from his wounds.

———————— ★ ————————

ALTHOUGH TRAIN TRAVEL was hardly new around Civil War times, it had steadily evolved from the early railroads of the 1820s. Passenger comfort was improving as well. Early on, tiny engines like the DeWitt Clinton, built in 1831 for the seventeen-mile Mohawk and Hudson Railroad, were used in trains designed with open passenger cars resembling stagecoaches, set just behind the engine.

★

THE BALTIMORE AND OHIO (B&O) RAILROAD opened in 1830, and the Pennsylvania Railroad connected Pittsburgh with the Atlantic coast. Later engines distributed the weight via several sets of wheels, were made to round the bends, and incorporated the boiler into the body of the engine. The transcontinental railroad was completed in 1869, and it continued to be the predominant means of transcontinental travel until well after World War II.

★

THE WORLD'S SHORTEST RAILROAD is in Dubuque, Iowa, and measures only 296 feet and has a 60-degree grade.

★

THE "GOLDEN" SPIKE wasn't really golden! Pure gold is far too soft to be pounded into a wooden railroad tie with a hammer, so builders used a spike that was made of an alloy of different metals, including gold, and covered in gold plating.

★

ELECTRIC TRACTION WAS introduced in 1895 for short stretches of railroad track, especially in urban areas when tunnels were involved. This electrification, which eliminated smoke and steam, was precipitated by a serious accident in New York City when a tunnel filled with smoke. Soon, trains passed under Park Avenue to enter Grand Central Terminal in Manhattan, in compliance with a state law discontinuing the use of combustion engines within New York City.

★

THE STAGECOACH WAS also a viable means of transportation in the West. The early railroads could only go so far. Manufactured in the quiet New England town of Concord, New Hampshire, the world-renowned Concord Coach became a symbol of the Wild West in the period following the Civil War. A durable coach, it could withstand harsh jolts on rutted roads, making it ideal for the wilderness.

★

WELLS, FARGO AND COMPANY, founded in 1852 to provide mail and banking services for the California gold camps, used stagecoaches as the fastest means of transportation for that part of the country.

★

IN 1861, ONE could buy a rail and stagecoach ticket, and barring any storms, floods, attacks by Native Americans, holdups, or breakdowns, might make it coast to coast in twenty-six days.

★

INVENTIONS SUCH AS the automatic coupler and the airbrake (invented by George Westinghouse) improved safety each decade. In the 1880s, Westinghouse pursued his interest in rail safety, and at the age of thirty-four founded Union Switch & Signal Company in Pittsburgh. Within two years, his company was selling complete systems for switching trains from track to track and indicating the position of every train.

JOHN AUGUSTUS ROEBLING, a German immigrant and civil engineer, left his mark in Pittsburgh and New York with his wire rope used to build suspension bridges. In 1857, Roebling designed and began construction of the Brooklyn Bridge, joining Manhattan with Brooklyn over the East River. Thousands celebrated its opening on May 24, 1883.

ONE OF THE most important strides came when George Pullman built a remarkable new railcar in 1864. These cars, given the name "Pullman cars," had sliding seats, upper berths, and comfortable heating. In addition, Fred Harvey, a Kansas restaurateur, introduced meals to the railroad.

IN 1894, PRESIDENT GROVER CLEVELAND sent federal troops to break up a strike by railroad workers at the Pullman Palace Car Company in Chicago because the strike over pay-cuts interfered with mail delivery.

AS THE RAILROAD PHENOMENON GREW, presidential campaigns adopted whistle-stop tours, in which the candidate would speak from the train's rear platform.

DURING WORLD WAR II, President Franklin D. Roosevelt used a specially built railcar with armor-plated sides and three-inch-thick bulletproof windows.

AFTER THE AMERICAN REVOLUTION, Revere devoted much time to making tea services in what's known as the Federal style. A genuine Revere item has the family name enclosed in a rectangle. Revere later worked in brass as well.

AMERICAN SHAKER CREATIONS originated with the Shakers, a Christian sect whose founder came from England. Since Shaker laws forbade anything too fancy, all creations, from buildings to furniture and baskets, were functional and unadorned. Light wood stains showed the natural beauty of the wood grain. By the 1880s, you could purchase Shaker replicas by mail order, especially chests, baskets, fabrics, and chairs.

ANOTHER FAMOUS AMERICAN ARTIST crafted beautiful stained-glass windows, bowls, and vases. Louis Comfort Tiffany had planned to become a painter, but he soon became known for his exquisite work in what he called favrile glass. This he created using a secret process of his own invention by which color, design, and texture are embedded into the glass before it is hand-blown. At the turn of the century, Tiffany art nouveau glassware was popular and would later become museum treasures.

———— ★ ————

IN 1869, THE first professional baseball team was organized. They called themselves the Cincinnati Red Stockings.

———— ★ ————

AARON MONTGOMERY WARD founded the first mail-order business in 1872. The Sears catalog didn't come along until 1886.

———— ★ ————

ALEXANDER GRAHAM BELL and repair mechanic Thomas Watson invented the telephone in 1876.

———— ★ ————

IN 1881, P.T. BARNUM teamed with James Bailey to form the Barnum & Bailey Circus.

———— ★ ————

ATLANTA DRUGGIST JOHN PEMBERTON invented Coca-Cola in 1886. The popular soft drink was first created as a health tonic.

———— ★ ————

IN 1895, Dr. John Harvey Kellogg invented the first flaked breakfast cereal.

ONE OF THE first major exponents of the Federal style, Charles Bulfinch designed the Massachusetts State House with its great, gold dome soaring high on Boston's Beacon Hill. It was one of the most distinguished public buildings when completed in 1798. Bulfinch also succeeded Benjamin Henry Latrobe as architect of the U.S. Capitol, completing it in 1830.

IN 1857, FREDERICK LAW OLMSTED, along with Calvert Vaux, originated and supervised the master plan for New York City's Central Park, the first major metropolitan park in a U.S. city. He also planned the grounds of the Capitol in Washington, DC, and was the first commissioner of Yosemite National Park in California.

CHAPTER 7

THE AGE OF INDUSTRY, INVENTION, AND DISCOVERY

When William McKinley was assassinated in 1901, Theodore Roosevelt became the youngest president at the age of forty-two. Full of energy and idealism, Roosevelt was well traveled and well read, and he loved strenuous exercise of all kinds. Raised in a wealthy family, he was also well connected, knowing many prominent business leaders. His image as a fairly ordinary citizen enhanced his appeal, and in turn, he championed the causes of the working class by maintaining a balance between wealthy industrialists, business owners, and ordinary workers. He inspired the nation to regain its former glory and this time allowed for fascinating products and discoveries made by the world's greatest thinkers, as you'll soon see in this chapter.

WHEN COAL MINERS in Pennsylvania went on strike for higher wages in 1902, President Roosevelt threatened to seize the mines if owners would not agree to arbitration. Similar actions earned him the moniker of "Trustbuster" when he acted to stop unfair practices in the big businesses of tobacco, oil, steel, and the railroads.

IN THE 1880s, Theodore Roosevelt established a working cattle ranch in the badlands of western North Dakota. Roosevelt spent three years working as a cowboy on his own ranch. He identified himself as a cowboy at heart for the rest of his life.

THE TOBACCO, OIL, STEEL, AND THE RAILROAD INDUSTRIES had established trusts, working together to limit competition. The most famous was the Standard Oil trust run by John D. Rockefeller.

THE SHERMAN ANTITRUST ACT OF 1890 regulated the operations of corporate trusts and declared that every contract, combination in the form of trust, or other act in restraint of trade was illegal. In the late 1990s, the Sherman Antitrust Act was used by the federal government to prosecute the Microsoft Corporation for abusing its monopoly power by combining its Internet Explorer Web browser software with its Windows operating system.

IN FEBRUARY 1902, Roosevelt brought suit under the Sherman Antitrust Act against the railroad trust of the Northern Securities Company. The people loved him for it, and when the case went before the Supreme Court, the decision came in five to four against the trust. Actually, the president did not want to disband all of these trusts—just the most flagrant ones. He called his moderate approach the "Square Deal."

LARGE FACTORIES HAD become the major employers for most people—a result of the Industrial Revolution at the end of the eighteenth century. But the downside to that was that workers lacked protection from almost all contingencies, including inflation, illness, disability, and arbitrary firing. Workers soon banded together, demanding a voice and a change in labor conditions. A secret fraternal order called the Knights of Labor embraced workers in many occupations, becoming one of the most powerful early unions.

IN 1881, WORKERS met in Columbus, Ohio, to establish a far more effective group called the American Federation of Labor (AFL). Its first leader was Samuel Gompers, president of the Cigar Makers' International Union and of the Federation of Organized Trades and Labor Unions. The AFL gave workers more rights, such as negotiating with employers for better conditions and wages.

IN 1892, LARGE numbers of private detectives as well as National Guard troops quelled striking workers at Carnegie Steel Company's Homestead Mill in Pittsburgh, essentially destroying the union.

PRESIDENT REAGAN WAS twice president of an actor's union, the Screen Actors Guild, which represents television and movies actors working in America. He is the only president of the United States to have also been head of a labor union.

IN 1894, a strike by the American Railway Union against the Pullman Company was defeated by an injunction issued under the Sherman Antitrust Act.

AFTER THE SPANISH-AMERICAN WAR, the trade union movement grew so that by 1904, more than 2 million workers belonged to trade unions. Almost 1.7 million belonged to the AFL. With great reluctance, employers gradually accepted collective bargaining with the unions as the norm.

IN THE EARLY 1900s, two brothers worked closely to develop early aeronautics. Wilbur Wright, along with his younger brother Orville, enjoyed constructing simple mechanical toys, and in 1888 they built a large printing press. The two soon began publishing a Dayton, Ohio, newspaper and opened a bicycle repair shop and showroom in 1892.

IN SEPTEMBER 1900, near Kitty Hawk, North Carolina, the Wright brothers tested their first glider invention, carefully noting their findings and correcting the problems they'd discovered. Astutely, they patented their idea and went on to construct their first propeller and a machine with a twelve-horsepower motor. At Kitty Hawk, on December 17, 1903, Orville Wright made the first test flight in their first powered glider, the Flyer I, making this the first airplane flight in history (though it only lasted a whopping twelve seconds).

ORVILLE WRIGHT'S FLIGHT on September 9, 1908 at Fort Myer, Virginia, established several records under government contract for a sixty-two-minute flight and made him an international celebrity.

FORD INTRODUCED the Model T in 1908. His first car sold for $850, a hefty sum back then. Ford developed an assembly-line style of manufacturing that became efficient enough to bring prices down. This assembly-line approach became the industry standard in the manufacture of automobiles. By the time the Model T (commonly known as the Tin Lizzy) was discontinued in 1927, its price of around $300 was widely affordable.

AT THIS TIME, there didn't seem to be anything a person couldn't buy from a Sears catalogue, including a house! Beginning in 1908, Sears offered to ship a customer a house ready to be assembled for anywhere from $100 to just over $600, depending on what kind of house the buyer wanted. Sears sold about 100,000 of these houses until it discontinued the program in 1940.

THE PANAMA CANAL connected the Atlantic and Pacific Oceans. Before it, ships had traveled from New York to San Francisco by taking the long route around Cape Horn at the southern tip of South America. Construction of the canal cut this journey by 7,000 miles.

THE PANAMA CANAL project became the most difficult undertaking during its time because of its complexity and its cost of $350 million.

THE FIFTY-MILE-LONG PANAMA CANAL opened to shipping on August 15, 1914, under United States control. Panamanian resentment over the next century led to new negotiations, and in the 1970s, treaties recognizing Panama's ultimate ownership of the canal and surrounding lands were signed. Panama controlled the region from 1979 on, and the United States officially turned over the Panama Canal in 1999.

THE SMITHSONIAN INSTITUTION stems from the generosity of James Smithson, a wealthy English scientist struck by the principles of the United States as well as the amazing discoveries made in our country in the nineteenth century. Upon his death in Italy in 1829, Smithson willed his fortune to his nephew, with the stipulation that if he died without heirs, the entire fortune would be given to the United States to create a fine institution where knowledge would be increased for future generations. President Andrew Polk signed a congressional act establishing the Smithsonian Institution, and construction began in the 1850s.

TODAY, THE SMITHSONIAN INSTITUTION is made up of sixteen smaller galleries on and off the National Mall and charges no admission, thanks to government funding and private donations.

ONE OF THE signers of the Declaration of Independence, Benjamin Rush founded the first public dispensary in Philadelphia and became one of the earliest doctors to characterize insanity as a medical condition rather than the influence of evil spirits. He was considered responsible for ending an epidemic of yellow fever in Philadelphia in 1793.

WHILE HE WAS revolutionary in many of his practices, Dr. Benjamin Rush still practiced bloodletting, an ancient and somewhat barbaric method of treating patients plagued by illness.

---★---

CRAWFORD WILLIAMSON LONG, a Georgia physician, was the first doctor to use ether (a gas that numbs pain but leaves the patient conscious) as a general anesthetic during surgery. William T.G. Morton was a Boston dentist who had publicly demonstrated ether as the first truly effective surgical anesthetic, but Dr. Long was the first to use it during an actual surgery: he painlessly removed a tumor from the neck of patient James M. Venable on March 30, 1842.

---★---

ELIZABETH BLACKWELL WAS America's first female physician. She graduated at the top of her class on January 23, 1849, and was the first woman to earn a degree in medicine in the United States. In spite of her accomplishments, American hospitals at the time refused to hire a woman, so in 1857 she founded her own clinic, the New York Infirmary for Indigent Women and Children.

---★---

MAJOR WALTER REED was a U.S. Army doctor who in 1900 confirmed the theory of Cuban scientist Carlos Finlay that certain mosquitoes spread yellow fever. This discovery saved thousands of lives during the construction of the Panama Canal (from 1904 to 1914).

---★---

MANY FAMOUS AMERICANS put their creativity to use discovering new processes and products, but none was as prolific as Thomas Edison, who patented 1,000 of his products, including incandescent electric light bulbs, the world's first large central electric-power station in New York City, and an alkaline, nickel, and iron storage battery.

———————— ★ ————————

ALTHOUGH HE WAS POPULAR, President Roosevelt knew he had never been elected to the post in which he now served. At first, it was unclear whether Roosevelt would win his Republican Party's nomination in 1904. However, the president was successful, winning not only the nomination, but also a landslide victory that stunned the incumbent president himself.

———————— ★ ————————

OF ALL OF the men ever to serve as president of the United States, only one has actually been able to claim our largest city as his hometown. Theodore Roosevelt is the only president ever to be born in New York City.

———————— ★ ————————

ON A BEAR HUNT in 1902, President Theodore Roosevelt found only a bear cub, which he couldn't bring himself to shoot. Upon hearing the story, the *Washington Post* ran a cartoon, inspiring a Brooklyn toy maker to place a copy of the cartoon in his window next to a stuffed brown bear. The term "teddy bear" stuck.

———————— ★ ————————

ROOSEVELT'S OLDEST CHILD, Alice, loved to shock people by smoking in public, keeping a pet snake, and behaving in other ways that were unconventional for women of that time, including betting on horses at the racetrack.

ROOSEVELT WAS the first president to invite an African American to dinner at the White House when he dined with Booker T. Washington, principal of the Tuskegee Institute in Alabama.

★

DURING THE CAMPAIGN OF 1904, Roosevelt vowed not to seek re-election in 1908. When the end of his second term rolled around, he wanted to stay in the position but chose instead to keep his promise. However, Roosevelt helped to pick his successor, William Howard Taft, who won the election of 1908.

★

WILLIAM HOWARD TAFT was the first president to buy automobiles for the White House.

★

TAFT WAS THE HEAVIEST president to date, weighing more than 300 pounds.

★

DUE TO HIS LARGE SIZE, Taft once got stuck in a White House bathtub! After being rescued from this embarrassing situation, Taft ordered that particular tub removed and oversaw the installation of a larger tub made to fit him. The new tub would comfortably fit four men of average size.

★

TAFT SERVED ONLY ONE TERM, but went on to become the tenth chief justice of the United States and the only person ever to hold the highest offices in both the executive and judicial branches.

———————— ★ ————————

DOLLAR DIPLOMACY WAS Taft's decision to use economic strategies (or "dollars"), such as having U.S. banks and companies invest in other countries, as a way to increase America's power and standing in the world.

———————— ★ ————————

THE AUTOMOBILE INDUSTRY remained in its infancy during World War I but quickly grew after 1918, leading to America's first real consumer buying spree.

———————— ★ ————————

AT STORES SUCH as Wanamaker's in Philadelphia, Macy's in New York City, and Marshall Field's in Chicago, Americans enjoyed boosting the economy. These large stores and catalog companies provided the goods consumers desired, and advertising entered the scene to create whatever desire didn't already exist. As prosperity spread in the Roaring Twenties, average Americans bought into the stock market, furthering the growth of newly merged companies and corporate giants.

———————— ★ ————————

THE NATIONAL ASSOCIATION for the Advancement of Colored People (NAACP) was founded in 1909 to champion the rights of African Americans, becoming the most influential black organization in America. Among early members were noteworthy Progressive Era individuals, including Jane Addams, Florence Kelley, William Du Bois (W.E.B. Du Bois),

John Dewey, Charles Darrow, Lincoln Steffens, Ray Stannard Baker, and Ida Bell Wells-Barnett.

SEVERAL INDUSTRIAL AND FINANCIAL POWER BROKERS arose in the early 1900s. Their drive, determination, and uncanny ability to see the future led to vast empires. These hallowed ranks include such legends as the Rockefellers and Andrew Carnegie, as well as some lesser-known names.

———— ★ ————

SON OF A PROMINENT INTERNATIONAL BANKER, J.P. Morgan began his career in banking and after the Civil War reorganized the railroads. By the end of the century, he controlled a transportation empire. In 1895, he founded J.P. Morgan & Co., which lent the U.S. government millions of dollars in gold. In 1901, Morgan organized U.S. Steel, the first billion-dollar corporation.

———— ★ ————

BORN IN SCOTLAND, Andrew Carnegie started life with no wealth to back his rise to power. When he came to America in 1848, he worked as a bobbin boy in a Pittsburgh cotton factory. But he moved forward as a messenger, telegrapher, and in various positions within the Pennsylvania Railroad. During his railroad rise, Carnegie invested in oil, iron, and bridge building. Carnegie, a savvy businessman and ferocious competitor, also became known for his philanthropy, giving away huge sums for future generations to enjoy.

———— ★ ————

IN THE 1870s, he concentrated on steel, and soon the Carnegie Steel Company became America's industrial giant.

—————————— ★ ——————————

JOHN D. ROCKEFELLER made his fortune with the Standard Oil Company, formed in 1870. During the 1880s, Rockefeller's Standard Oil Trust controlled virtually all of the nation's refineries. Not surprisingly, antitrust sentiments prevailed, and as the trust dissolved, Rockefeller formed Standard Oil of New Jersey as a holding company until the Supreme Court broke it up in 1911. Rockefeller retired early, his personal wealth a staggering $1 billion.

—————————— ★ ——————————

UPON HIS FATHER'S RETIREMENT IN 1911, John D. Rockefeller Jr. assumed the reins in business. He also led the board of directors of the Rockefeller Foundation (among other board posts), and in 1930, he began supervising a massive undertaking in New York City. It was an extensive complex of buildings, completed in 1939, known as Rockefeller Center, or Radio City, where the ice rink and Christmas celebrations remain prominent today. Rockefeller's philanthropy extended also to New York City land given to the United Nations (upon which the international headquarters was established) and to the restoration of Colonial Williamsburg in Virginia.

—————————— ★ ——————————

EDWARD H. HARRIMAN was born to wealth, but he built his fortune even further. Success on Wall Street led Harriman to rebuild bankrupt railroads in 1881. The centerpiece of this effort was the Union Pacific Railroad, but he also acquired controlling shares in other lines.

—————————— ★ ——————————

BORN A CANADIAN, James J. Hill matched financial wits with some of the finest in business. In the United States in the late 1870s, Hill became a partner in the St. Paul and Pacific Railroad, which he acquired along with other lines. In time he consolidated his holdings into the Great Northern Railway.

— ★ —

HILL AND J.P. MORGAN paired against Harriman and financier Jacob Schiff in a battle for the Northern Pacific Railroad, causing tremors in the stock market in 1901.

— ★ —

THE TRADITION OF NEWSPAPERS vying for readers based on their divergent perspectives dates back to Thomas Jefferson and Alexander Hamilton, who each found newspaper forums to use as their sounding boards.

— ★ —

UNTIL THE 1830s, newspapers were published essentially for the elite, but as printing techniques improved, the number of papers grew. In 1833, Benjamin Day founded the *Sun* in New York; the *New York Morning Herald* followed in 1835, founded by James Gordon Bennett. These two competing dailies led to the creation of a news gathering force known later as the Associated Press.

— ★ —

THE FIRST MODERN GAME OF BASEBALL was played in 1846. Incredibly, it wasn't until April 15, 1947, that Jackie Robinson became the first African American to play baseball in the major leagues, breaking the "color line"—a practice of racial segregation dating to the nineteenth century.

— ★ —

IN THE EARLY 1900s, Edward Wyllis Scripps formed the United Press Association, which in 1958, after a merger with International News Services, became United Press International.

— ★ —

BY 1850, MONTHLY magazines such as *Harper's Monthly*, the *Atlantic*, and the *Ladies' Home Journal* informed and entertained Americans. You could buy the *Saturday Evening Post* for a nickel by the end of the century. Around this time, a young California upstart made himself a success with the *San Francisco Examiner*, which he took over from his father. With this newspaper, William Randolph Hearst intended to take on another successful publisher, Joseph Pulitzer, whose newspaper empire (starting with the *New York World*) reached beyond New York City.

JOSEPH PULITZER HAD pioneered the newspaper business with the advent of the sports pages, women's fashion section, and more.

HEARST AND PULITZER tried to outdo each other from the comics to coverage of scandals, bringing forth the term "yellow journalism" to describe the sensational techniques often used to attract readers.

JOSEPH PULITZER DONATED $1 million to Columbia University for a school of journalism, founded in 1912, and funded Pulitzer Prizes.

PRESIDENT KENNEDY IS the only American president to ever win the Pulitzer Prize.

ADOLPH OCHS KEPT steering his newspaper, the *New York Times*, founded in 1851, to serious news coverage with the slogan "All the news that's fit to print."

TABLOIDS BEGAN AROUND 1919 as more easy-to-read newspapers profusely filled with illustrations and graphics. The *New York Daily News* was one of the first, followed by Hearst's *Daily Mirror*.

ON MAY 5, 1906, a powerful earthquake measuring 7.9 on the Richter scale rocked San Francisco, causing three days of raging fires that destroyed many downtown and residential areas. Fortunately, San Francisco was quickly rebuilt and hosted the Panama-Pacific International Exposition in 1915.

BY 1922, *Reader's Digest* truly capitalized on the reading and news phenomenon. Published by DeWitt and Lila Acheson Wallace, this small magazine featured informative but condensed articles that had previously appeared elsewhere. It remains successful with that tradition into the twenty-first century. The Digest, as some call it, inspired other magazine upstarts such as *Time* and *Newsweek*, and in 1925, the *New Yorker*, with its fine fiction, articles, and cartoons. *Life* hit newsstands in 1936 and proved that pictures could tell a story as well as words.

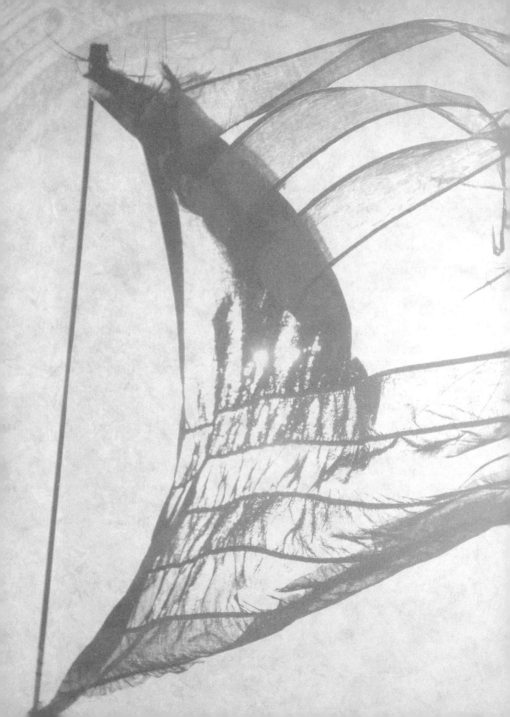

CHAPTER 8

WORLD WAR I AND THE GREAT DEPRESSION

The son of a Presbyterian minister, Woodrow Wilson took the presidential oath of office in 1913 determined to live up to his new commitment. Indeed, his high moral principles were tested, for it took much skill to keep the United States at peace in a world moving toward war. World War I (also known as "The War to End All Wars," and "The Great War") raged in Europe from 1914 to 1918, and resulted in the end of the Austro-Hungarian, German, Ottoman, and Russian Empires.

After the devastating war, the 1929 stock market crash sent Americans plummeting into the Great Depression, though the war was by no means the only reason why the nation faced an economic downturn. During Prohibition, bootlegging made money for organized crime figures and even more respectable businessmen, but it did little for the national economy. For nearly a century, single-crop farming had ruined the soil and contributed to cycles of drought and flooding in America's farm belt. Finally, the unequal distribution of wealth and surpluses in business corporations meant that farmers and laborers were not able to purchase the goods being produced.

IN JUNE 1914, Austro-Hungarian archduke Francis Ferdinand and his wife were assassinated by Serbian nationalists as they rode through the streets of Sarajevo in Bosnia. It provoked hostilities in Europe and fostered the combat readiness of many armies put on alert.

———————— ★ ————————

RUSSIA, AS THE PROTECTOR OF GREEK-ORTHODOX CHRISTIANS, feared that Austria intended to annex Serbia and wanted to settle the issue in the Hague Tribunal (a court of arbitration). Austria refused. Germany backed Austria, for the two countries were allies.

———————— ★ ————————

ON JULY 28, 1914, Austria declared war on Serbia, and this caused Russia, an ally of Serbia, to mobilize. Germany sent an ultimatum to Russia to halt its mobilization or face German action. Russia refused, and Germany then declared war on Russia on August 1. As if this wasn't enough wrangling between world powers, France, a Russian ally, refused to urge the Russians to stop. France wanted to regain the Alsace-Lorraine region, which it had lost to Germany in the Franco-Prussian War of 1870–71. Germany declared war on France on August 3, and also invaded Luxembourg and Belgium.

———————— ★ ————————

FEW REALIZE THAT World War I was fought between countries whose rulers were relatives. King George V of England was the first cousin of Kaiser Wilheim of Germany and Czar Nicholas II of Russia. Queen Victoria, grandmother to these royal children, was their determined matchmaker, believing that if she arranged international marriages it would help bring about world peace.

———————— ★ ————————

THE FRENCH JOINED the fighting, and the Austro-Hungarian Empire declared war on Russia in August 1914. President Wilson was committed to neutrality while the other countries began to fight the Great War, named World War I years later. Eventually thirty-two nations became embroiled in the conflict.

---- ★ ----

IN WORLD WAR I, the French-British-Russian alliance became known as the Allied Forces. Germany and Austria-Hungary formed the Central Powers.

---- ★ ----

BRITAIN'S SEA POWER had effectively halted German shipping, but this created problems for the United States, which had supplied food and arms to both sides. The British tightened their blockade, and as Germany's supply routes were closed off, the Germans faced starvation unless they worked around it.

---- ★ ----

BY APRIL 1917, more than $2 billion worth of goods had been sold by the United States to England and the Allied countries. The German navy used submarines, called U-boats, to torpedo vessels supplying England. Unfortunately, this included U.S. ships.

---- ★ ----

WHILE THE GERMAN embassy had issued a warning to travelers to cross the Atlantic at their own risk, many gave little heed to that admonition. Only one passenger canceled his ticket of all the vessels that were traveling.

---- ★ ----

IN APRIL 1915, the British Cunard liner *Lusitania* prepared to leave New York harbor. On May 7, the *Lusitania* was passing Ireland on its way to England when a German submarine attacked, sinking the ship with 1,198 passengers onboard, including 126 Americans. Germany insisted that the *Lusitania* carried munitions; the United States denied the allegations (though it would later be learned that there were cases of shells, cartridges, and small-arms ammunition onboard).

EVEN THOUGH THE ship's sinking enraged Americans, who felt the Germans had attacked a defenseless civilian vessel, the Wilson administration was determined to keep the country out of war. The United States forced Germany to modify its method of submarine warfare, but in no time at all, the Germans sunk a French steamer, causing the loss of additional American lives.

WILSON WON RE-ELECTION in 1916 while the war in Europe raged on.

ALTHOUGH MANY FORMER presidents are buried at the National Cemetery, which is near the national capital of Washington, DC, there is only one president buried in Washington, DC: Woodrow Wilson, who is buried at the Bethlehem Chapel of the Washington Cathedral. He passed away on February 3, 1924.

THE NUMBERS OF casualties mounted: in the Battle of the Somme, 1.25 million men on both sides were killed, wounded, or captured; the Battle of Verdun resulted in 1 million French and German casualties.

WILSON WARNED THE GERMAN COMMAND of the United States' strong opposition to unrestricted submarine warfare. Therefore, when Germany announced that, effective February 1, 1917, unrestricted submarine warfare would be launched on all shipping to Great Britain, the president had little choice but to break off diplomatic relations. At Wilson's request, a number of Latin American countries also broke off relations with Germany.

★

IN A SPEECH BEFORE CONGRESS, Wilson suggested that if American ships were attacked, he would be forced to act. Not heeding the U.S. signals, the Germans sent secret telegrams to Mexico promising an alliance in return for help in defeating the United States should it enter the war. The British intercepted a telegram from Arthur Zimmerman, the German foreign minister to Mexico, which encouraged Mexican attacks upon the United States, offering the return of Arizona, Texas, and New Mexico in exchange.

★

THE RED SCARE resulted in America's obsession with Communism following the Bolshevik Revolution in 1917. In 1919, the U.S. House of Representatives refused to seat Socialist representative from Wisconsin, Victor L. Berger, because of his socialism, German ancestry, and antiwar views.

★

GERMAN U-BOATS TORPEDOED two American ships (the *Illinois* and the *City of Memphis*) on March 16, 1917, and Wilson asked Congress to declare war. The United States officially declared war on Germany on April 6, 1917.

★

GENERAL JOHN PERSHING, having led the force that took on Mexican revolutionary Pancho Villa in New Mexico, was given command of American expeditionary forces in Europe. But unlike its allies, the United States had no large standing army to send overseas, nor was the nation equipped with planes, ships, and other military equipment.

———————— ★ ————————

UNLIKE THE CIVIL WAR, no one could buy his way out of military service in this conflict. Thus, the first American troops arrived in France in June 1917—approximately 200,000 Americans in training.

———————— ★ ————————

AMERICANS BEGAN LEARNING about poison gas, hand grenades, and demolition when they went to war. Trench warfare provided some basic protection against enemy fire, but not nearly enough. Enemy soldiers raided the trenches, killing unsuspecting soldiers, and the mud and dampness wreaked havoc on the soldiers' health. Penicillin and other antibiotics didn't exist, so even minor cuts were potentially lethal.

———————— ★ ————————

THE TIDE WAS starting to turn against the Germans. They had failed to destroy the British navy through submarine warfare and began sustaining heavy losses in their U-boat fleet, around the same time the Allies' shipbuilding efforts increased. In December 1917, Russia signed a peace agreement with the Austro-German negotiators, essentially ending eastern-front fighting.

———————— ★ ————————

THE RUSSIAN REVOLUTION had occurred after Czar Nicholas II abdicated in March. Withdrawal from the Great War was a cardinal point in Bolshevik policy.

IN JANUARY 1918, President Wilson proposed his peace plan, but the war continued.

IN MAY, ALLIED VICTORY came in the tiny French village of Cantigny as Americans, in their first offensive of the war, took the town in less than an hour, aiding their British and French counterparts.

THE GERMANS LAUNCHED a major offensive along the Chemin des Dames Ridge, and the Americans defeated the Germans at Belleau Wood, a small hunting ground, in June. In fact, U.S. artillery hit Belleau with everything it had, ravaging the area with shells and fire.

NEITHER THE BRITISH nor the German press (including official dispatches) were forthcoming in their reports of the war. The title of Erich Maria Remarque's great novel, *Im Westen nichts Neues* (*All Quiet on the Western Front*) was a German army dispatch on a day when thousands of soldiers were dying in the trench warfare of World War I.

ON SEPTEMBER 26, 1918, American and French troops launched the Meuse-Argonne offensive in an effort to cut off the Germans between the Meuse River and the Argonne Forest, and British forces breached the Hindenburg line the next day. The Germans had fortified this line for four years, reinforcing bunkers with concrete and turning towns into virtual forts.

DESPITE THE PREPARATIONS by the Germans, the fresh supply of Allied troops, combined with overhead fighting power, overwhelmed them. It took much forward movement and military strategy on land, in the air, and through naval blockade, but the Hindenburg line was broken on October 5, sealing Allied supremacy. The Allies were gaining on the enemy. By November 1918, the American Expeditionary Forces numbered nearly 2 million.

ON NOVEMBER 11, 1918, Germany and the Allies reached an armistice agreement, thus ending years of heavy fighting and world rancor.

MANY OF THOSE who'd survived the war died of influenza as a worldwide epidemic struck. But victory was at hand. From January through June of 1919, the Allies discussed the treaty, which came to be known as the Treaty of Versailles. Members of the Big Four—Georges Clemenceau of France, Vittorio Orlando of Italy, David Lloyd George of Britain, and Woodrow Wilson of the United States—met in the Hall of Mirrors at the French palace.

THE TREATY OF VERSAILLES changed the map of Europe. One provision was the formation of a League of Nations, based on President Wilson's ideas to achieve lasting peace and world justice. However, for the League of Nations to truly effect peace, it required all members' assistance. If some withheld their cooperation, the league had no way of enforcing its will.

———— ★ ————

THE ALLIES GAVE Germany the ultimatum to either sign the Treaty of Versailles agreement or return to battle. As a result, protests broke out in Germany and Hungary, but Germany was strong-armed into signing the treaty. Although the Treaty of Versailles solved some of Europe's problems, it created others; the Allies had come to Versailles looking to extract the cost of the war from the Central Powers.

---- ★ ----

THE UNITED STATES Senate didn't ratify the treaty, and the United States didn't join the League of Nations—this alone guaranteed the League's failure.

---- ★ ----

THE FOURTEEN POINTS was the name given to the proposals of President Woodrow Wilson to establish a lasting peace following the Allied victory in World War I. Wilson outlined these points in his address to a joint session of Congress in January 1918, giving further evidence of his moral leadership.

---- ★ ----

OHIO HAS SUPPLIED more presidents to our country than any other state, eight presidents in all! Aside from William Henry Harrison (who was born in Virginia, and moved to Ohio when it was still a territory), all of these presidents were born and raised in Ohio: Ulysses S. Grant, Rutherford B. Hayes, James A. Garfield, Benjamin Harrison, William McKinley, William Howard Taft, and Warren G. Harding.

---- ★ ----

AS THE NEW DECADE BEGAN, Warren G. Harding took over the presidency after campaigning to return America to normalcy. On November 2, 1920, radio station KDKA in Pittsburgh broadcast the presidential election results. This spawned not only a new industry, but also a new way to disseminate news about the nation, its leaders, and its current events.

———————— ★ ————————

WARREN G. HARDING was the first president to address the nation using radio broadcasts.

———————— ★ ————————

HARDING'S TRUSTED ADVISORS sullied the administration with numerous scandals. But before Harding could be impeached for any wrongdoing, he died in office in 1923, amid speculation of foul play.

———————— ★ ————————

THE TEAPOT DOME was the most famous of Harding's scandals. Interior Secretary Albert Fall was convicted of selling oil from the U.S. Navy's huge oil reserve at Teapot Dome, Wyoming, and pocketing the money received for it (he also got a herd of cattle as part of the deal). He served ten months in jail.

———————— ★ ————————

CALVIN COOLIDGE TOOK the oath of office and restored trust in the executive branch after Harding's death.

———————— ★ ————————

ONE DAY WHILE COOLIDGE WAS PRESIDENT, his wife was too ill to go to church on Sunday. Coolidge went without her. When they sat down to dinner that night, Mrs. Coolidge was feeling better and wanted to talk about the sermon she had missed earlier that day. She asked her husband what the subject of the minister's sermon had been that morning. Known as a tight-lipped man, all Coolidge said was, "Sin." That answer didn't satisfy his wife, and she pressed him to tell her what the minister had said about sin. "He was against it," was Coolidge's reply.

———————— ★ ————————

THE TEAPOT DOME SCANDAL, named after an oil field in Wyoming, involved United States Secretary of the Interior Albert B. Fall leasing the rights to public oil fields to private oil companies (without competitive bidding) in exchange for thousands of dollars. Fall was found guilty and sentenced to one year in prison, making him the first cabinet member to go to jail for his actions while in office.

———————— ★ ————————

THE ROARING TWENTIES received this distinction because of the outrageousness of the times. Prohibition restricted many people's lifestyles, tempting them to disobey the law. Illegal "speakeasy" bars flourished, along with gangsters and organized crime.

———————— ★ ————————

THE 1920s SERVED as the golden era for New York theater, which in prior decades had consisted of farces, melodramas, and musicals, but nothing of much literary merit. The time spawned playwrights such as Eugene O'Neill and Noel Coward.

———————— ★ ————————

A NEW STYLE of music hit the nation with its African American folk rhythms combined with popular and European music. W. C. Handy, a black musician, was unable to attract a music publisher for his song "St. Louis Blues," so he published it himself in 1914. Forever after, his sound was known as jazz.

THE JAZZ ERA, which many say first took hold in New Orleans, flourished with talented musicians such as Louis Armstrong. As African Americans migrated north for better industrial jobs, it caught hold in Chicago and in Harlem, a section of New York City that was undergoing its own renaissance.

AFTER KDKA BROADCAST the election results, radio took hold. Prior to World War I, amateur operators in dozens of cities regularly transmitted music and speech, but the war ended all that. In 1925, WSM Radio in Nashville, Tennessee, began airing barn dance music, which would later become known as the Grand Ole Opry. In 1927, Congress expanded the Radio Act of 1912 to reflect this new industry, no longer run by amateurs but by commercial enterprises.

IN 1934, THE industry created the Federal Communications Commission (FCC) to consider license applications and renewals for radio stations. The FCC also set guidelines for obscenity and false claims in advertising.

FOR YEARS THE Anti-Saloon League of America (ASL) had urged saloonkeepers to give up their businesses. By 1900, millions of men and women regarded drinking alcoholic beverages as a dangerous threat to families and society. On December 22, 1917, Congress submitted to the states the Eighteenth Amendment, which prohibited "the manufacture, sale, or transportation of intoxicating liquors." By January 1919, ratification was complete.

THE 1925 TRIAL of a biology teacher named John Scopes, who had been arrested for teaching theories of evolution that contradicted the biblical version of creation, was another famous broadcasting moment.

WHETHER SCOPES RECEIVED a fair trial (a prayer opened each court session, and expert evolutionists were banned from taking the stand) is unclear. Scopes was found guilty, but was fined only $100. The Tennessee Supreme Court later overturned the local court's decision, citing a technicality. Although it never reached the U.S. Supreme Court, the Scopes trial served to showcase many freedoms in the Bill of Rights—the freedoms of speech, religion, and the separation of church and state.

THE 1924 IMMIGRATION ACT became another controversial political issue stemming from the Red Scare, for it set quotas on the number of immigrants allowed into the United States. Congress limited immigration to 2 percent of each nationality present in the United States in the year 1880. This year was chosen mainly because at that time there were very few people of Far Eastern and East European descent present in the United States, thus severely limiting further influx.

--- ★ ---

THE IMMIGRATION ACT of 1965 put an end to national quotas for immigration, making individual talents and skills or close relationships with U.S. citizens a better basis for admittance.

--- ★ ---

WOMEN'S RIGHTS IN the 1800s were very limited—husbands had the legal right to exercise total authority over their wives. Married women couldn't retain their own wages, control their own property, or even keep custody of their children if they sought a divorce.

--- ★ ---

IN THE PROSPEROUS POSTWAR ERA, women stashed conservative clothing in their closets and wore dresses that clung to their bodies and skirts above the knee. Such fashionable women became known as "flappers." They cut their hair shorter in a "bobbed" style and enjoyed a new sense of freedom not granted to prior generations of young ladies. These women were the first to smoke and the first to dance "wildly" with the Charleston, popular at that time.

--- ★ ---

WOMEN ALSO BEGAN to enter careers beyond the limits of nursing or teaching during this time, for typewriting skills yielded further job prospects for millions of women—far more than worked around the turn of the century.

--- ★ ---

EMMA WILLARD, self-taught in algebra, geometry, geography, and history, tutored young ladies and petitioned the New York legislature to open a girls' school. She didn't stop there, though; her strides led to female teachers, more competitive salaries, and financing for women's education.

--- ★ ---

WOMEN WHO HAD tremendous impact throughout American history include Frances Perkins, the first female cabinet member as secretary of labor during Franklin D. Roosevelt's administration; Jeannette Rankin, the first woman to serve in Congress; and Shirley Chisholm, the first African American woman to serve in Congress.

--- ★ ---

THOUGH OBERLIN COLLEGE in Ohio had been the first in America to admit women in 1837, Mount Holyoke Female Seminary in South Hadley, Massachusetts, carried out Willard's educational philosophy. Mount Holyoke was founded by Mary Lyon the same year as Oberlin College.

--- ★ ---

ELIZABETH CADY STANTON began crusading as an abolitionist, but her work furthered women's rights as well. Stanton joined Lucretia Coffin Mott, Lucy Stone, and Susan B. Anthony in speaking out in favor of a woman's right to vote, a right once granted by some colonies in Colonial America but lost years later.

--- ★ ---

CARRIE CHAPMAN CATT proved to be a talented organizer and served as president of the National American Woman Suffrage Association.

--- ★ ---

THESE WOMEN REFORMERS became known as suffragettes, and the American suffragist movement scored its major achievement following the victory in World War I.

IN 1919, CONGRESS approved the Nineteenth Amendment providing that "the right of citizens of the United States to vote shall not be denied or abridged by the United States or by any State on account of sex." The amendment was ratified August 18, 1920.

ANOTHER IMPORTANT EFFORT benefiting women was Margaret Sanger's crusade for contraceptives and the newly coined phrase "birth control." As a nurse in some of the poorer sections of New York City, Sanger saw women overburdened with more children than they could care for. She believed that oversized families spawned poverty, and that in any case, women should have rights over their own bodies.

SANGER OPENED the country's first birth control clinic in Brooklyn in 1916, but those who viewed her activities and the information she disseminated as obscene thwarted her efforts. But Sanger wasn't deterred easily, and in 1952, she persuaded a friend to back research that ultimately led to "the pill," or oral contraceptives.

IT WAS NOT until 1965 that the U.S. Supreme Court invalidated Connecticut's law banning the dissemination of birth control information and prescriptions.

THE POPULARITY OF Washington Irving and James Fenimore Cooper proved in the 1800s that Americans craved quality literature. Irving's *The Sketch Book* contained stories such as "Rip Van Winkle" and "The Legend of Sleepy Hollow." Its subsequent publication in London made Irving the first internationally recognized American writer.

EARLY AMERICAN LITERATURE had begun in New England, but with the success of Irving and Cooper, New York became the literary center of America.

A FEW WRITERS known as the Concord Group, mostly followers of Ralph Waldo Emerson, put New England back on the literary map. Emerson and other transcendentalists maintained steadfast opposition to the overemphasis on material progress. Henry David Thoreau embraced much of this in his work, especially in his most famous book, *Walden*, describing the two years that he spent living as a virtual recluse in a simple cabin on the banks of Walden Pond, near Concord, Massachusetts.

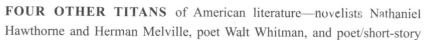

FOUR OTHER TITANS of American literature—novelists Nathaniel Hawthorne and Herman Melville, poet Walt Whitman, and poet/short-story writer Edgar Allan Poe—defined the craft of writing.

EDGAR ALLAN POE, a desperate man with bouts of alcoholism, depression, and unemployment, wrote some of his best work (including the mysterious and the macabre) just to survive, such as the detective story "The Murders in the Rue Morgue." It was the publication of *The Raven and Other Poems*, however, that set him apart as an internationally acclaimed poet.

—— ★ ——

WALT WHITMAN WROTE in rhythmic free verse about controversial subjects, but in many cases espoused democratic ideals. He self-published *Leaves of Grass* in 1855 as a collection of twelve long poems.

—— ★ ——

ON MAY 21, 1927, Charles Lindbergh became famous for the first solo transatlantic flight from New York to Paris, which took thirty-three hours and thirty minutes.

—— ★ ——

LINDBERGH WAS AWARDED the Congressional Medal of Honor and in 1954, he earned a Pulitzer Prize for his book bearing the same name as his plane, *The Spirit of St. Louis.*

—— ★ ——

MARK TWAIN of Missouri came to public notice with *The Adventures of Tom Sawyer, The Adventures of Huckleberry Finn*, and his autobiographical *Life on the Mississippi.*

—— ★ ——

MARK TWAIN'S REAL name was Samuel Clemens.

—— ★ ——

EMILY DICKINSON WAS reticent in life (indeed, she lived out much of her life as a recluse in her Amherst, Massachusetts, home), but after her death she came to be regarded as one of America's finest poets.

—————— ★ ——————

IN THE POSTWAR PROSPERITY, some writers yearned to return to the simpler life with basic values. These were known as "the Lost Generation." Ernest Hemingway was one of them, and his novels *The Sun Also Rises* and *A Farewell to Arms* both appeared in the late 1920s.

—————— ★ ——————

IN 1954, HEMINGWAY received the Nobel Prize for literature, but sadly, he succumbed to severe depression and alcoholism and committed suicide in 1961.

—————— ★ ——————

T.S. ELIOT, another of the Lost Generation, was awarded the Nobel Prize for literature in 1948.

—————— ★ ——————

SINCLAIR LEWIS CHRONICLED the career of a corrupt evangelist in *Elmer Gantry* and became the first American writer to win the Nobel Prize, which he was awarded in 1930.

—————— ★ ——————

PEARL S. BUCK was the first woman to win the Nobel Prize for Literature, in 1938. *The Good Earth*, a novel about a northern Chinese peasant family, is considered to be her masterwork.

—————— ★ ——————

THE NYSE BEGAN in 1792 when a group of stock and bond brokers gathered in downtown New York City to trade stocks, bonds, and other instruments of finance. Two years later, the trading moved indoors on the corner of Wall and Water Streets. Then in 1817, the exchange moved closer to its present Wall Street location. It drew up a more formal constitution and soon became the country's center of finance. In 1863, it became known as the NYSE.

THROUGHOUT THE 1920s, Americans speculated in stocks in record numbers. When they didn't have the disposable cash, they invested their life savings as well as borrowed money. Those who were highly leveraged lost everything when market jitters began on October 24, 1929. The massive selling spree of millions of shares collapsed businesses and sent investors and brokers scrambling.

ON OCTOBER 29, 1929, the market hit bottom. "Black Tuesday," the single worst day for the NYSE, was largely thought to have caused the Great Depression, but truly the economy was growing at a rate that was far too fast to sustain. Another cause was increased industrialization and wealth remaining in the hands of a few.

THROUGHOUT PROHIBITION, drought in the Midwest, and increasing economic inequality, three presidents—popularly known as the "do-nothing presidents"—avoided any government intervention, preferring to let business and its leaders take care of their own affairs. These three presidents were Warren G. Harding, Calvin Coolidge, and Herbert Hoover, who had been elected in 1928.

PRESIDENT HOOVER WAS the first Quaker president of the United States. Quakers are forbidden by their religion from supporting or participating in war or any other acts of violence. This is called *pacifism*. Hoover himself was not a pacifist. He thought that war was acceptable if waged in defense of one's country.

THE ONCE-ORPHANED HOOVER was a self-made businessman and a millionaire, and plenty of voters saw him as the quintessential American success story. Hoover had even distributed food as Wilson's national food administrator in World War I. But as the effects of the Depression deepened, many unfairly blamed Hoover and lost faith in his policies of economic isolationism.

OTHER NATIONS, such as Great Britain, were reaching out to the poor with payments to the unemployed and the elderly. Most Americans began to believe that their own government owed them some form of assistance. But President Hoover, though sympathetic, held fast to his principle of individual responsibility.

CLEARLY, HOOVER FAILED to grasp the extent and severity of the problem. When in March 1930 he claimed that the worst was just about over, the unemployment rate rose, more businesses failed, banks closed, and many people defaulted on their mortgages and lost their homes.

CONGRESS TRIED TO respond to the economic crisis with the Smoot-Hawley Tariff Act of 1930 that raised tariff rates to record levels. Although hesitant to put his name on the legislation, President Hoover signed it anyway. The intention was to increase sales of U.S. products by raising the cost of imported goods, but the measure was a miserable failure. An international trade war broke out, drastically reducing sales of U.S.-made goods overseas. As international trade was weakened, foreign countries plunged into what was now a worldwide depression.

---- ★ ----

BY 1932, APPROXIMATELY 12 MILLION PEOPLE were out of work compared to 4 million two years before.

BECAUSE OF THE president's lack of government assistance, his name was given to the growing wretched shantytowns—called "Hoovervilles"—while those who had only newspapers to protect them from the cold were said to use "Hoover blankets." The president once hailed for his humanitarian gestures was now ridiculed for his failure to help the American people.

---- ★ ----

IN MAY 1932, thousands of World War I veterans, once promised a bonus from the army, walked, rode the rails, or otherwise made their way to the nation's capital to demand the payment, which they needed immediately, not in the mid-1940s when the payments were scheduled to occur. Congress turned them down, and that July, Hoover lost patience with the contingent of former soldiers and ordered the standing U.S. Army, led by General Douglas MacArthur, to drive them away with tear gas.

---- ★ ----

WHEN FRANKLIN ROOSEVELT got married in 1905, it was a family affair in more ways than one. Wealthy Americans at the time had a habit of marrying distant cousins (so distant that they were really related in name only). Roosevelt's own father and mother were sixth cousins. He married his fifth cousin, Anna Eleanor Roosevelt, and another fifth cousin, President Theodore Roosevelt, gave the bride away (he was her uncle).

FACING THE 1932 ELECTION, the Republicans didn't want to take the blame for the Depression, and so they renominated Hoover as their candidate. The Democrats chose Franklin Delano Roosevelt, who had first earned a seat in Congress from New York in 1910 as a liberal Democrat.

FRANKLIN DELANO ROOSEVELT had been crippled by polio in 1921. Though he made progress with his recovery, Roosevelt would forever be confined to a wheelchair (however, since it was before the advent of television, most Americans were not aware of this). The public rarely saw him sitting in a wheelchair or using the steel braces he needed to walk. By common, unspoken consent, the press almost never photographed Roosevelt while he was in motion.

FDR'S POLIO STRUGGLE transformed this wealthy New Yorker into a champion of the poor and downtrodden. Roosevelt's campaign slogan stated "Happy Days Are Here Again," and he won the election.

IN HIS INAUGURAL ADDRESS, Roosevelt reassured the nation when he said, "The only thing we have to fear is fear itself." He also pledged that he would ask Congress for broad executive power "to wage a war against the emergency, as great as the power that would be given to me if we were in fact to be invaded by a foreign foe."

ON INAUGURATION DAY, many states had declared bank holidays in order to keep the remaining banks solvent. They feared the runs on the banking system that had already occurred with depositors lining up to withdraw their money. Two days later, on March 6, President Roosevelt called a halt to banking operations, and three days later Congress, which had been called to special session, passed the Emergency Banking Act. Federal auditors examined bankbooks, unsound banks would be closed, and approximately 12,000 banks were back in business.

IN NOVEMBER 1933, the Twenty-first Amendment repealed Prohibition. Most Americans heralded its passage (though the state of Utah was the last to ratify it). In the decade prior, Prohibition had only led to bootlegging, smuggling, and an increase in organized crime. In addition, the economic crisis created a demand for federal revenues from the taxation of alcohol.

ROOSEVELT FOLLOWED UP with massive reform as Congress established the Federal Deposit Insurance Corporation (FDIC) in 1933, which guaranteed individual deposits up to $5,000 (that amount has increased over time). The new law, just as the president had intended, gave investors the confidence that if the bank failed, they wouldn't lose all their funds.

TWO ACTS, one in 1933 and another the following year, brought forth detailed regulations for the securities market, enforced by the newly created Securities and Exchange Commission (SEC). Joseph P. Kennedy became the commission's first chairman.

THE FEDERAL EMERGENCY RELIEF ADMINISTRATION (FERA) was created in 1933 and led by Roosevelt's trusted advisor Harry Hopkins. The FERA made initial cash payments to the unemployed, but also put people to work in jobs that didn't compete with private enterprise.

---★---

THE AGRICULTURAL ADJUSTMENT ACT was a complex farm bill that paid farmers to take land out of cultivation. It had been intended to raise agricultural prices, and in 1936 it was declared unconstitutional by the U.S. Supreme Court.

---★---

ONE OF THE MOST PROFOUND New Deal programs stemmed from passage of the Social Security Act of August 1935. This legislation consisted of three core components—a retirement fund for the elderly, unemployment insurance, and welfare grants for local distribution (which included aid for dependent children). Social Security was developed in the United States later than in several European countries, which had instituted such programs before World War I.

---★---

TWO YEARS AFTER the Social Security program was passed into law, 21 million workers were covered by unemployment insurance and 36 million were entitled to old-age pensions.

———————— ★ ————————

THE TENNESSEE VALLEY AUTHORITY (TVA) was particularly innovative, building dams in seven southeastern states to generate electricity and manage flood control programs. Power came to thousands in rural regions where electricity had not previously been delivered.

———————— ★ ————————

PERHAPS THE CORNERSTONE of the New Deal was the National Industrial Recovery Act passed in 1933 to establish the National Recovery Administration (NRA). It was supposed to encourage good business by establishing codes of fair competition. Workers were to be guaranteed such things as minimum wages, maximum hours, and the right to collective bargaining. Unfortunately, code making got way out of hand, resulting in hundreds of codes for various industries. Its director, the former army officer Hugh S. Johnson, resigned after failing to win over the American people, and in 1935, the Supreme Court declared the NRA unconstitutional.

———————— ★ ————————

THE NEW DEAL seemed to be off to a rousing start, for in the first hundred days of the new administration there was a flurry of legislation to get the country moving forward again. Public works projects put thousands on the job, creating infrastructure such as the Lincoln Tunnel connecting New York with New Jersey, as well as the Golden Gate Bridge in San Francisco. Whatever political opposition the president faced was taken care of in 1934 when Democrats swept the midterm elections, increasing their majorities in both the Senate and the House.

--- ★ ---

THE MANY BANK failures in the Great Depression caused the United States Congress to create an institution that would guarantee bank deposits. The Federal Deposit Insurance Corporation (FDIC) was created by the Glass-Steagall Act of 1933. The FDIC currently guarantees checking and savings deposits in member banks up to $100,000 per depositor.

--- ★ ---

THE WORKS PROGRESS ADMINISTRATION (WPA) provided government funding not only for building construction, but also for artists and writers. As a result, murals were painted, plays performed, photographs taken, and folk music sung. Through the Federal Writers Project, state-by-state guidebooks were created, while the Federal Theater Project staged free performances.

ROOSEVELT'S BRAIN TRUST was instrumental in the passage of his unprecedented array of social programs. The individuals forming this advisory group consisted of government outsiders, including professors, lawyers, and economic experts. The enduring legacy of the New Deal was government's increased involvement in the lives of its citizens.

--- ★ ---

JOHN L. LEWIS rose to power in the organized labor movement. In 1935, he founded the Committee for Industrial Organization (CIO) that broke with the American Federation of Labor (AFL) to become the most radical labor organization in the country.

--- ★ ---

HUEY LONG, GOVERNOR OF LOUISIANA, became one of the most controversial politicians. Nicknamed "Kingfish," he improved roads and expanded services in his state by taxing corporations and the rich. In 1931, he resigned as governor to enter the U.S. Senate, where he developed the Share-Our-Wealth program, promising to make "every man a king."

LONG HAD PLANNED to run for president in 1936, but was gunned down a year earlier at the height of his political influence.

IN 1935, CONGRESS passed the National Labor Relations Act, known as the Wagner Act (for Senator Robert Wagner of New York, its sponsor). The act established the National Labor Relations Board (NLRB). This law guaranteed workers the right to organize and bargain through unions. Frances Perkins, the first female cabinet member, served as secretary of labor during this time.

BONNIE AND CLYDE, Baby Face Nelson, Pretty Boy Floyd, and John Dillinger fascinated the public. Though they were all gangsters who lived and died by the gun, people couldn't learn enough about them. Dillinger, for instance, was wanted by J. Edgar Hoover and the Bureau of Investigation (today's Federal Bureau of Investigation, or FBI).

ONE OF DILLINGER'S most famous acts was his 1933 escape from jail using a mock gun carved from wood. A year later, he coerced a plastic surgeon to alter his face and fingerprints, but the "feds" caught up with Dillinger, shooting him outside a movie theater.

AMELIA EARHART WAS the first woman to fly across the Atlantic. She challenged herself and set several other records. But in 1937, she took off on an around-the-world trip with a navigator, never to return. Her plane simply vanished, and despite a massive search, no trace of her was found.

MUSICIANS OF THE TIMES, including Count Basie, Duke Ellington, Ella Fitzgerald, and Louis Armstrong, had hit songs during the 1930s. Oddly enough, the same establishments who spun their records most likely would not have served these African Americans on account of segregation. Shunning prejudiced attitudes, Big Band leader Benny Goodman toured with a racially integrated band.

RADIO CONTINUED TO capture Americans who desperately needed an escape. Popular programs of the day included *The Jack Benny Show*, *Fibber McGee and Molly*, *The Edgar Bergen/Charlie McCarthy Show*, and *The Shadow*. Orson Welles popularized *The Shadow*.

IN 1938, ORSON WELLES produced a radio broadcast based on H.G. Wells's science fiction classic *The War of the Worlds*, in which Martians invaded a New Jersey town (in the novel, the Martians invaded several English towns). He pulled off the production with such realism the night before Halloween that some spooked listeners panicked, believing the broadcast was indeed an actual news report of an invasion from outer space.

THE RADIO BROADCAST of *The War of the Worlds* caused listeners to jam up highways hoping to escape the aliens and beg police for gas masks to save them from the toxic gas. There were even rumors that the show caused suicides, but none were ever confirmed.

★

JESSE OWENS CAPTURED headlines with his four-medal performance at the Summer Olympics in 1936. Owens, a U.S. sprinter, won the two sprint events as well as the long jump. Berlin, Germany, hosted that year's games.

★

CHARLIE CHAPLIN AND Mary Pickford had appeared in early silent movies, but now the technology continued to evolve with the invention of Technicolor (a three-color process) on the big screen. Alfred Hitchcock thrillers were all the rage, and so was the comedy of Laurel and Hardy and movies starring Jimmy Stewart, Clark Gable, Mae West, and the young Shirley Temple. Movie theaters provided not only entertainment, but information as well, since many learned their current events from the newsreels that chronicled headlines and images from around the world.

★

WILLIAM LE BARON JENNEY, American architect and engineer, pioneered the use of metal-frame construction for large buildings. He used cast-iron columns encased in masonry to support steel beams bearing floor weights. Freed from bearing the load, outside walls could be filled with windows. Jenney's revolutionary construction method spurred the emergence of skyscrapers.

★

FINISHED IN 1902, the Flatiron Building at Fifth Avenue and Twenty-third Street was Manhattan's first skyscraper, standing approximately 312 feet tall. In 1930, architect William Van Alen added the art deco Chrysler Building to the skyline.

IN 1931, the Empire State Building was completed on Fifth Avenue, between Thirty-third and Thirty-fourth Street, making it the tallest building in the world at that time (1,250 feet), 202 feet taller than the Chrysler Building.

EVEN THOUGH IT no longer holds the distinction of the tallest building, with its elegant art deco design, the Empire State Building is regarded as the quintessential American skyscraper. It featured prominently in the 1933 movie *King Kong*, where the creature climbed the Empire State Building (actually, he climbed a model used for the sequence).

CHAPTER 9

WORLD WAR II

The Treaty of Versailles had disarmed the German military and replaced the kaiser with a democratic government, for which Germany had no previous model. The League of Nations lacked the ability to act decisively, for it required unanimous opinion (always hard to obtain, but particularly tough with feuding nations). In addition, when financial markets around the world collapsed, the German mark was devalued. The Russian Revolution popularized Communism and other antidemocratic philosophies. As if that weren't enough, fascism was gaining influence in many countries, but particularly in Italy. While you may think you know all there is to know about World War II, this chapter will provide you with the details your textbooks and history professors missed while teaching this tragic period of history.

IN GERMANY, THE National Socialist (Nazi) Party was attracting attention between 1929 and 1931. The first Nazis, a rather bitter group of German World War I veterans, blamed their defeat on the Communists and German Jews.

———————— ★ ————————

BY 1932, the Nazi Party wielded considerable power in the German parliament (called the Reichstag). German President Paul von Hindenburg was growing weak in his advanced years.

———————— ★ ————————

ADOLF HITLER, known for his racial hatred and contempt for democracy, took advantage of the situation and won a following that placed him in a position to ascend to power. Hitler gained the chancellorship in January of 1933 and became dictator three months later.

———————— ★ ————————

BEFORE VON HINDENBURG'S DEATH, Hitler had already ordered the killings of high-ranking Germans whom he saw as a threat to his power. Books that contained thoughts contrary to the Nazi beliefs were burned.

———————— ★ ————————

THE *HINDENBURG*, a German airship that began transatlantic passenger service in 1936, was a source of Nazi pride. But on May 6, 1937, as it approached Lakehurst, New Jersey, the dirigible burst into flames and crashed, killing many onboard and one person on the ground.

———————— ★ ————————

DEFYING THE TREATY OF VERSAILLES, Germany had left the League of Nations the year before. The country also began its rearmament, again defying the treaty. Most Allies, along with the League of Nations, stood idly by as the new dictator sent troops to the demilitarized zone.

★

THE PRIME MINISTER and dictator of Italy, Benito Mussolini, was an ally of Hitler and also a Fascist. He invaded the country of Ethiopia on the African continent in October of 1935.

★

ADOLF HITLER WAS maniacal in his obsession with creating a pure master race that had no traces of Jewish influence, and no place for the handicapped, the independent thinker, and certainly not for the Jew.

★

MEIN KAMPF (*My Struggle*) written by Adolf Hitler in the mid-1920s was part autobiography and part political ideology of Nazism.

★

IN 1935, HITLER'S NUREMBERG DECREES forbade Jews from marrying nonJews. They could not hold government positions, and they were barred from practicing law or medicine. They could no longer attend German universities.

★

HITLER'S POLICE FORCE (called the Gestapo, a branch of the Schutzstaffel, or SS for short) began rounding up Jews and other supposed undesirables, who were then sent to forced labor camps. Those able to work were used to build roads or provide other manual labor, but the rest were exterminated in camps, such as Auschwitz in Poland.

———————— ★ ————————

NAZI GERMANY AND FASCIST ITALY made their alliance formal in 1936 with the Rome-Berlin Axis. Meanwhile, the Empire of Japan aligned with Germany against Communism, and Italy followed suit.

———————— ★ ————————

IN 1938, HITLER INVADED AUSTRIA, annexing it to his Third Reich. Not satisfied, he went after the Sudetenland in Czechoslovakia, demanding its annexation.

———————— ★ ————————

THE TREATY OF VERSAILLES had formed Czechoslovakia at the conclusion of World War I.

———————— ★ ————————

FRANCE AND BRITAIN, based on the terms of a treaty, should have defended the Sudetenland, but to pacify Hitler and avoid conflict they didn't oppose his aggression. In fact, British Prime Minister Neville Chamberlain returned to Britain in 1938 with Hitler's signature on the Munich Pact, guaranteeing what Chamberlain called "peace in our time."

———————— ★ ————————

WHILE GERMANY DECLARED war on the world, the Spanish Civil War erupted. Factions, one led by Generalissimo Francisco Franco, struggled from 1936 to 1939. Hitler and Mussolini aided Franco as if they were practicing for larger conflicts to come. Again, countries—including the United States— remained neutral, though Soviet dictator Joseph Stalin provided military aid to Franco's opposition in Spain.

———————— ★ ————————

PROVING HE COULDN'T BE TRUSTED, one year later in 1939, Hitler seized the rest of Czechoslovakia, followed by a portion of Lithuania. During this same period, Mussolini took Albania.

———————— ★ ————————

THE TREATY OF VERSAILLES had given part of German territory to Poland, an area known as the Polish Corridor. When Germany rolled tanks into the Polish Corridor with massive force on September 1, 1939, France and Britain could no longer watch from the sidelines. They'd had enough. World War II had erupted.

———————— ★ ————————

THE GERMANS INVITED the Soviets into Poland from the east in early September 1939, and by September 6, the Polish government fled Warsaw. Dividing Poland between Germany and Russia made it look as if there were an alliance between the two countries. Indeed, the Soviet Union and Germany had signed a nonaggression pact in 1939. However, Hitler had long desired to conquer European Russia. The pact simply bought him some time.

———————— ★ ————————

THE FRENCH HELD fast to the Maginot Line, a series of strong fortifications built in the 1930s along the Franco-German frontier to ensure that Germans stayed on their side. The line ran from Switzerland to the Belgium-Luxembourg border and into the south of France. At one end lay the Ardennes Forest.

PUTTING THEIR TRUST in Germany that the Maginot Line would be honored, the French had not crossed it either. Believing Hitler's army would attack through Belgium over the open plains, France and Britain mobilized to meet the German troops east of Brussels. Germany, however, chose to invade France through the dense forests of the Ardennes, cutting off the British and French armies in Belgium. Hitler's strategy was to push through the Ardennes toward Boulogne, Calais, and Dunkirk.

HAVING ESCAPED TO London across the Channel, General Charles de Gaulle put together a Free French government in exile while Jean Moulin held together the Resistance movement within France. The Gestapo (Geheime Staatspolizei, or secret state police) arrested Moulin in 1943. Torture by his German captors led to his death.

AT THE BEGINNING of the war, the Royal Air Force in Great Britain was besieged by German air attacks as Hitler attempted to control British airspace for his planned invasion. Terrified Londoners had crowded into underground subways for protection from the nightly bombing. Hitler later abandoned his invasion plans, but torpedoed supply ships, attempting to starve the island nation into surrender.

FDR DID EVERYTHING in his power to help the beleaguered British. He lent them fifty or sixty destroyers for their own protection, even though the United States (at the time) was maintaining its position of neutrality.

WAR ALSO RAGED throughout Africa, but it was fought mostly by Italy, Germany, and Britain, along with a few American forces. When Allied forces made their way onto the Mediterranean shores of Morocco and Algeria, they hoped to cut off German lines. But the landings were politically tricky because under terms of the French-German armistice, the North African French colonies were now in the hands of the Vichy French government (a puppet government while the Free French worked in the Resistance). Defending the colonies would have poised them against Allied soldiers. But as hoped, the Allies met with only slight resistance coming ashore.

NATIONALISM HAD GROWN in Japan during the 1930s just as it had in Germany. Loyalty toward Emperor Hirohito was drilled into young children, who revered the man not only as a leader, but as a god. When Japan attacked China to expand its territory, it found itself fighting not one but two governments—the Chinese Nationalists, led by Chiang Kai-shek, as well as the Chinese Communists with their leader Mao Tse-tung. America preferred the Nationalists, yet was determined to remain neutral.

RELATIONS BETWEEN the United States and the Japanese had weakened prior to the Pearl Harbor attack. The United States, along with much of the rest of the world, had condemned the expansion of Japanese power in Asia and the South Pacific. Government officials believed a Japanese attack was fairly imminent, but strongly suspected that it would occur in the South Pacific islands (such as the Philippines).

AS THE JAPANESE attacked Oahu in 1941, the new radar technology had detected blips on the screen, but Americans believed they were U.S. aircraft.

THE USS *ARIZONA* MEMORIAL was established to honor the servicemen who perished during the surprise attack on December 7, 1941. More than 1,000 sailors went down with the sunken ship and remain buried at sea. The hull lies about forty feet beneath the memorial and can be seen from above.

THE PEARL HARBOR ATTACK crippled nearly all of the U.S. battleships, with the *Arizona* exploding into a blaze five stories high. Four-fifths of her crew died instantly. The only vessels to escape the onslaught were two aircraft carriers, which had been at sea—the *Lexington* and the *Enterprise*. These two ships would soon have surprises of their own for the Japanese.

DURING THE PEARL HARBOR ATTACK, nineteen naval vessels were either sunk or badly damaged and nearly 200 army and navy planes were shot down. Over 2,400 Americans (including 68 civilians) were killed and over 1,000 wounded.

IN 1940, FDR MADE HISTORY, for never before had a president served longer than two terms, or eight years. President Roosevelt's leadership was pulling the nation out of its economic depths, and the public rewarded him with a third term.

***

MANY AMERICANS BELIEVED that the oceans on either side of the American continent would protect it from war. Many of them, including the prominent Charles Lindbergh, spoke out in an organization called America First, filled with isolationists who wished to prevent U.S. entry into the growing conflict.

***

ON DECEMBER 7, 1941, Japanese dive-bombers and torpedo planes launched a surprise early-morning attack on the U.S. naval base at Pearl Harbor, Hawaii (then a territory). The air raid sank most of the American Pacific fleet of ships and destroyed aircraft on the ground. It also killed more than 2,300 servicemen and nearly 100 civilians. President Roosevelt, reflecting the mood of an outraged nation, called on Congress the next day.

***

THREE DAYS AFTER the Hawaiian attack, Germany and Italy declared war on the United States. Suddenly thrust into the Second World War, Americans found themselves immersed in the war effort.

***

DURING THE EARLY MONTHS OF 1942, more than 100,000 Japanese Americans (though they were U.S. citizens) found themselves relocated into internment camps. Anti-Japanese sentiment crossed to hysteria as these citizens were forced to leave their homes and jobs to live under the harsh conditions of the camps. It's reported that President Roosevelt opposed this relocation measure, but that he bowed to public pressure. After he was re-elected in 1944, Roosevelt ordered the camps closed.

---- ★ ----

AFTER THE BOMBING OF PEARL HARBOR, the United States engaged the Empire of Japan in several battles across the South Pacific. In particular, the Battle of the Coral Sea (fought in early May, 1942) was a turning point that effectively checked the Japanese advance to the south. Admiral Chester Nimitz, privy to decoded enemy messages of the Japanese, tried to thwart their plans to cut off Australia. The *USS Lexington* was sunk and the *USS Yorktown* damaged. The Japanese retired from this battle with heavy losses.

---- ★ ----

IN JUNE 1942, U.S. carriers ambushed Japanese carriers descending on the Midway Islands. Four Japanese carriers were sunk. The U.S. victory at Midway dashed any Japanese hopes to invade Hawaii. Coming on the heels of the Battle of the Coral Sea, it gave the United States supremacy at sea in the South Pacific.

---- ★ ----

GUADALCANAL, THE LARGEST ISLAND of the Solomon Islands not far from Australia, was the site of heavy fighting as the Japanese occupied the Solomons in January 1942. On August 7, U.S. Marines launched the first of their amphibious assaults on the enemy, fighting in the jungles until February 1943, when they secured the island.

PART OF THE Northern Mariana Islands, Saipan is an island in the South Pacific. In early 1944, American forces pounded Japanese garrisons, then in June landed army and marine troops, who fought a three-week campaign. Victory here was crucial, as it would put the island of Japan within range of U.S. bombers. The island could accommodate bases for long-range bombers, but an invasion of Japan would have to wait until Germany was defeated.

★

GENERAL MACARTHUR HAD promised the Filipino people in 1942 that he'd return to liberate the Philippine Islands, for which Japan fought aggressively. If the United States took them back, Japan's oil supply in the East Indies would be in great jeopardy. From this position, the United States could target its bombs on Japanese industrial centers.

★

GENERAL MACARTHUR'S TROOPS landed on Biak Island on May 27, 1944. From there U.S. planes could attack the Japanese fleet in the Philippines. Several Japanese battleships and three aircraft carriers fell victim to U.S. submarines, including one prize—the *Shokaku*, which had participated in the Pearl Harbor raid. The invasion of the Philippines brought the Japanese navy out in force for the last time.

★

DURING THE THREE-DAY Battle for Leyte Gulf in October 1944, the Japanese lost twenty-six ships, including an enormous battleship, while the Americans only lost seven ships. MacArthur's pledge was fulfilled.

★

THOUGH A TINY volcanic island merely five miles long, Biak Island's airstrips were vital for American short-range aircraft targeting Japan. Air strikes preceded the U.S. Marines' landing on February 19, 1945. The brutal struggle was unlike anything Europe had seen. More than 6,000 U.S. Marines lost their lives capturing the island from the Japanese (whose losses were estimated at 20,000). The campaign concluded on March 16 of that year.

ON APRIL 1, 1945, the United States launched a massive amphibious assault on the Japanese island of Okinawa. The U.S. Navy, protecting the landings, came under kamikaze (suicide air raid) assault. It was a savage land battle with eighty-two days of fighting.

U.S. FORCES SUFFERED over 72,000 casualties, and the Japanese forces lost about 66,000 in fighting on Okinawa. In addition, over 122,000 Japanese civilians were killed.

SURPRISING HITLER and Mussolini, the Allies struck Sicily in early July 1943. At this point, the Italian army had lost the will to fight. Mussolini was arrested but later rescued by Hitler, who poured in fresh troops to maintain control of the Italian peninsula. Though the Italians surrendered in September 1943, fighting within Italy would continue. The Allies liberated Rome on June 5, 1944.

WHEN SOLDIERS DROPPED from parachutes during the D-day invasion, they were so scattered about on land that in order to identify one another as Allied forces they used clicker devices that made the sound of a cricket. This way, they could remain fairly quiet before facing enemy forces.

★

DUBBED OPERATION OVERLORD (a name coined by Winston Churchill), the invasion of France would take place in Normandy on what the Allies termed "D-day." Amphibious forces from the United States, Canada, and Britain would storm five beaches code-named Utah, Omaha (both stormed by American troops), Juno (stormed by Canadian troops), Sword, and Gold (both stormed by British troops). Three airborne divisions would also be dropped to protect the invading troops.

★

THE "D-DAY" MISSION called for just the right weather conditions to be successful. Severe wind and rain postponed the crossing by one day. General Eisenhower okayed the invasion to begin on June 6 when the weather cooperated.

★

THE ALLIES KNEW they could not linger on the beaches, for Hitler had promised swift retaliation if they tried to invade France. As the Normandy beaches were secured, it was no longer necessary to use artificial harbors (called "Mulberries") because Cherbourg was a genuine port, allowing replacements and supplies ashore. Fighting at Caen left that ancient town a pile of rubble, but on August 25, the Allies marched triumphantly through the streets of Paris.

★

AFTER U.S. AND BRITISH FORCES landed in North Africa, they suffered defeats in Tunisia around 1942. The Kasserine Pass was an important gateway to Algeria. Fortunately, the Germans were low on supplies, and their general called off further fighting. German and Italian forces surrendered in North Africa in May 1943, allowing the Allies to focus on the European continent.

IN LATE 1942 through early 1943, Battle of Stalingrad nearly destroyed most of the men and military might of Germany and Russia. Stalingrad was a strategically located industrial center and a vital German target. After heavy fighting, the Germans could no longer sustain their losses, and the Soviets were able to prevail. There ended the German advance into the USSR, though much of Stalingrad was destroyed. Thus, the Soviets moved the Germans west while the other Allied armies drove the Germans east, pushing them back to the Rhine.

AFTER THE NORMANDY INVASION, Allied forces swept through France but stalled along the German border that September. From intelligence reports, the Allies realized that the Germans were within striking distance of Antwerp. A particularly harsh winter also hindered defense efforts. In December 1944, General George Patton pushed his troops through Bastogne, Belgium, in forty-eight hours, a feat others swore he couldn't manage. The Allied success took weeks to accomplish, with the help of air power pushing the Germans back to their own lines in January.

AS THE ALLIES closed in on the German frontier, Hitler surprised them with an attack through the Ardennes Forest. Hitler reasoned that if the Germans cut off Allied supplies at Antwerp, Belgium, it would prevent their moving into his homeland. German troops fooled the weary Allies by dressing in G.I. uniforms. Poor weather had rendered Allied aircraft useless.

THE GERMANS HAD hoped to stop the Allies as they crossed the Rhine, but American forces used the Ludendorff Bridge, which the Germans had failed to destroy. The Red Army pushed toward Berlin. The Soviets reached Berlin on April 22, 1945 but it took another ten days for the city of Berlin to surrender.

★

IN 1945, Hitler had ordered that even children mount a defense against the Americans and Soviets. Hitler's SS squads (the secret state police) publicly executed anyone refusing to obey and fight.

★

AS ALLIED TROOPS battled to liberate Caen in July 1944, Hitler's officers, believing the führer was insane, plotted to assassinate him. One staff member was poised to take over to form a new government. But a heavy desk saved Hitler when the conspirators' bomb exploded during a meeting.

★

THE EXTRAORDINARY MILITARY SKILL of Field Marshal General Erwin Rommel of Germany, who had led the German forces in Africa, earned him the moniker "the Desert Fox." He was among those who committed suicide after the failed attempt to assassinate Hitler.

★

ON APRIL 30, 1945, Hitler and his new wife, Eva Braun, realizing that Berlin was finally falling, committed suicide in the bunker where they had lived for the past six months. The Nazis burned their bodies. Hitler's Third Reich was literally reduced to ashes.

★

AFTER THE AMERICANS and Soviets converged in Germany in April 1945, Berlin fell to the Allies at the month's end. As his last significant act before his suicide, Hitler named Grand Admiral Karl Doenitz to succeed him as chief of state. Though loyal to the führer, Doenitz had no other course but to surrender. General Alfred Jodl, Doenitz's representative, signed the surrender document at Eisenhower's headquarters in Reims on May 7.

THE FULL AND UNCONDITIONAL SURRENDER took effect at one minute past midnight after a second signing in Berlin with Soviet participation. May 8, 1945, would forever after be known as V-E Day, short for Victory in Europe.

ON THE HOMEFRONT, AMERICANS rallied together to support the war effort. The increased industrialization certainly stimulated the sluggish economy, which was climbing out of the Great Depression. As military production rose, and with men conscripted into the armed services, women took jobs or volunteered in staffing weapon factories. This quickly earned females the moniker "Rosie the Riveter."

THE EMERGENCY OFFICE OF PRICE ADMINISTRATION (OPA) was created to oversee the rationing of, among other things, automobiles and tires, leather shoes, farm machinery, typewriters, bicycles, gasoline, home heating oil, coal, coffee, sugar, and meat. In fact, the government instituted a thirty-five-mile-per-hour speed limit aimed at conserving tires and gasoline. Speeders were not looked on too kindly and were viewed as unlawful and unpatriotic. Rationing was undertaken in conjunction with price and rent controls as well.

WOMEN, ACCUSTOMED TO wearing nylon or silk stockings, had to do without these to ration after World War II. Some drew a black line down the back of their legs with an eyebrow pencil to give the appearance of a seamed stocking. Of course, where there is limited supply and great demand, the illegal or black market flourishes. Ration coupons, stamps, and certificates were used for items in short supply.

★

MANY AMERICAN FAMILIES planted victory gardens in their back yards to supplement their diets after the war, allowing commercial farms to supply food for the troops. The war provided the impetus some farmers needed to experiment with crop rotation and better fertilizers.

★

THE SOLE SURVIVOR POLICY is a set of regulations that protects members of a family from the draft or combat duty if they have already lost family members in military service. The regulations were a response to the loss of the five Sullivan brothers who were all killed when the *USS Juneau* was sunk during World War II.

★

IN 1944, CONGRESS passed the Servicemen's Readjustment Act, better known as the "G.I. Bill." This was essentially a benefits package for returning veterans that spawned a postwar baby and housing boom. It established veterans' hospitals around the country where vets could obtain rehabilitation and medical care and provided low-interest mortgages, college tuition, and trade-school funds.

★

LEADERS AT THE YALTA CONFERENCE called for a conference of nations to promote world peace and cooperation following the war. On April 25, 1945, delegates from fifty nations met in San Francisco to draft a charter. The charter was ratified by the U.S. Senate on July 28, 1945. The United Nations (UN), with its home in New York City, was adopted on October 24, 1945, to foster better relations and encourage respect for human rights. Member nations pledged to settle differences peacefully.

AS IF EXHAUSTED by his efforts overseeing the war, Franklin Delano Roosevelt died of natural causes at his home in Warm Springs, Georgia, in April 1945. Sadly, the man whose administration was plagued by the actions of Hitler and the Japanese died before any surrender or victory.

VICE PRESIDENT HARRY S. TRUMAN was sworn in as the nation's thirty-third president on April 12, 1945.

PRESIDENT TRUMAN DIDN'T have an actual middle name. He was named for his mother's brother, Harrison Young. Truman's parents couldn't make up their minds whether to give him a middle name of Solomon, after his mother's father, Solomon Young, or Shippe, after his father's father, Anderson Shippe Truman. So they compromised and just listed his middle name as S, without even a period afterward.

IN 1932, BRITISH SCIENTIST JAMES CHADWICK discovered an atomic particle, the neutron, which could penetrate the nucleus of an atom and cause it to separate. The divided atom would release more neutrons, causing other atoms to split. As the chain reaction progressed and built up, an enormous amount of energy would be released.

——————— ★ ———————

DURING THE FIRST DAYS OF WORLD WAR II, leading physicists such as Albert Einstein suspected that Germany was already at work to create a massive weapon of annihilation, better known as the atomic bomb or A-bomb. In 1939, Einstein collaborated with several physicists in writing to President Roosevelt to warn him of possible German attempts to make the atomic bomb. This lent urgency to American efforts to build the A-bomb, but Einstein played no role in the work and had no knowledge of what would be called the Manhattan Project.

——————— ★ ———————

IN 1942, MANY prominent scientists began developing the A-bomb in a small Tennessee community (as well as in research sites such as Los Alamos, New Mexico). The undertaking was termed "the Manhattan Project" because some of the work took place at Columbia University.

——————— ★ ———————

PHYSICISTS ENRICO FERMI and J. Robert Oppenheimer worked on the Manhattan Project, as did chemist Harold Urey. U.S. Army engineer General Leslie Groves headed the project that at one time involved approximately 600,000 people.

——————— ★ ———————

OAK RIDGE, TENNESSEE (near Knoxville), originally called Clinton Engineer Works, was founded in 1942 by the U.S. government to produce the uranium for the Manhattan Project. By the end of the war, the town's population had grown to more than 80,000.

---★---

AFTER V-E DAY, the war in the Pacific theater still raged on. American bombing raids on Japan's industrial centers met with limited success. With the Manhattan Project, U.S. scientists proved they could use the explosive power of nuclear fission rather than TNT to wreak mass destruction. Although the bomb had originally been created for possible use against Hitler's Third Reich, Truman used the A-bomb on the Japanese.

---★---

OPPENHEIMER AND HIS team tested the A-bomb near Alamogordo, New Mexico, on July 16, 1945. No one knew whether it would work until a tremendous blast rushed across the desert. Oppenheimer's team informed President Truman that it had indeed worked.

---★---

AT 8:15 A.M. ON AUGUST 6, 1945, an American B-29 bomber named the *Enola Gay* ferried the bomb to Hiroshima, the Japanese city chosen for the drop. There, it exploded about 2,000 feet above the ground, producing a fireball hotter than the surface of the sun and leveling several square miles. Atomic radiation and searing heat vaporized everything in its range.

---★---

JAPAN DIDN'T ASK for terms of surrender following the attack on Hiroshima. So on August 9, another B-29 bomber dropped an A-bomb on the city of Nagasaki, causing almost as much destruction as the first bombing.

---★---

THE SOVIET UNION had declared war on Japan on August 8, destroying its army in China and taking over most of occupied Manchuria. The Red Army was continuing its move into Korea as Japan finally surrendered to the Allies on August 15, 1945.

JAPAN'S SURRENDER AFTER the bombing on Nagasaki wasn't unconditional, as the Allies agreed that the Japanese could keep their emperor. The formal signing took place on September 2 in Tokyo Bay aboard the battleship *Missouri* with an American delegation headed by General MacArthur, who then became the military governor of Allied-occupied Japan.

IN OCTOBER 1945, a tribunal of French, British, Russian, and American judges indicted more than twenty individuals for war crimes and atrocities committed during World War II. These charges included the instigation of war, the extermination of ethnic and religious groups, the murder and mistreatment of prisoners of war, and deportation of hundreds of thousands to slave labor in lands Germany occupied. A number of high-ranking members of the Nazi party were charged. The event was called The Nuremberg Trials.

THE NUREMBERG TRIALS began on November 20, 1945. The persecution used much of the evidence that Allies discovered after the war. Twelve defendants were sentenced to death by hanging, seven received lengthy prison sentences ranging from ten years to life, and three were acquitted. At the conclusion of the first trial, twelve additional trials occurred in which approximately 185 others were indicted, including doctors who performed medical experiments in concentration camps as well as SS officials.

AFTER THE WAR, parts of Germany occupied by France, Great Britain, and the United States were allowed to merge, forming the Federal Republic of Germany (FRG), commonly called West Germany.

★

THE EASTERN PART OF GERMANY occupied by the Soviets became the German Democratic Republic (GDR), better known as East Germany, after World War II.

★

BERLIN, THE CAPITAL of prewar Germany, had suffered much damage and was situated in East Germany. Subsequently it was divided into four parts—each controlled by the United States, Britain, France, and the Soviet Union.

★

IN 1945, WEST BERLIN (controlled by the United States, Britain, and France) became a Western-ruled island until East Germany fell in 1990. This division symbolized the collapse of the German Empire and represented the tension evidenced in the Cold War between communist and free nations in the decades ahead.

★

IT WASN'T UNTIL 1961 that a physical barrier—the Berlin Wall—was erected to block free access in both directions. From the time the wall was built until it was torn down in October 1990, following Germany's reunification, about eighty people died attempting to cross from East to West Berlin.

★

EUROPE LAY IN ruins after the six-year-long war. Without a prosperous European continent, the United States might have suffered another severe economic depression. The U.S. program of financial assistance to help rebuild these devastated countries was called "the European Recovery Program." Today, it's better known as the Marshall Plan, after U.S. Secretary of State George Marshall.

★

LEADERS IN 1947 met in Paris to discuss the Marshall Plan, but when the Soviets realized that the United States wanted their cooperation with the capitalist societies of Western Europe, they left the meeting to establish their own plan to integrate Communist states in Eastern Europe. With more than $13 billion in U.S. aid to Western Europe, there was clearly an economic curtain dividing it from the Soviet-backed lands.

★

THE LARGEST AMOUNTS of aid after World War II went to Great Britain, France, Italy, and West Germany, respectively.

★

TRUMAN BELIEVED THE United States had to assist Greece and Turkey when Communist rebels threatened their security. He expressed these beliefs in a dramatic appearance before a joint session of Congress on March 12, 1947. His policy of containing communism whenever possible became known as the Truman Doctrine.

1950s–1970s

One of the most significant effects of World War II was felt over the long term: a shift in the world balance of power. In the 1950s, Britain and France (Allied countries) as well as Germany and Japan (Axis enemies) ceased to be great military powers, leaving only the United States and the Soviet Union (USSR) as leaders with the weapons to prove their might.

The evolving decade of the sixties would produce a different kind of power struggle between the government and its citizens. The civil rights revolution would gather greater force and speed; a youth culture no longer willing to accept the status quo would question authority and demand answers; sexual, drug, and feminist revolutions would further change American society; and finally, a war in Vietnam would divide the country and create wounds that would take decades to heal.

Efforts to end the war in Vietnam and return veterans to U.S. soil continued through the 1970s. Richard Nixon had won the 1968 election on his campaign promise to end the war, though he was helped by the opposing party's disarray. As the years passed, President Nixon became increasingly paranoid. He resented the antiwar movement, and he used his power and influence to intimidate those he saw as enemies. As time wore on, his list of enemies seemed to grow substantially larger.

DURING THE 1940s, President Truman ordered the investigation of applicants for government jobs for fear of communist infiltration. Both the Central Intelligence Agency and the National Security Council were created to focus on new security and intelligence issues.

———————— ★ ————————

IN 1948, AMERICAN writer and editor Whittaker Chambers testified before Representative Richard Nixon and the House Un-American Activities Committee that he'd been a Communist in the 1920s and 1930s, and that he'd transmitted secret information to Soviet agents. He charged that Alger Hiss, a member of the State Department, was a Communist and that Hiss turned over classified documents to him. Although Hiss denied the charges, Chambers produced document copies implicating Hiss in the matter. After a probe by the Department of Justice, Hiss was indicted for perjury. His first jury failed to reach a verdict, but his second trial in January 1950 handed him a conviction.

———————— ★ ————————

COMMUNISM WAS TAKING hold in China as well, where the Nationalist government of Chiang Kai-shek (which the United States had supported) could no longer withstand the onslaught of Communist forces led by Mao Tse-tung (now often spelled "Mao Zedong"). By the end of 1949, government troops had been defeated, forcing Chiang into exile on Taiwan. Elated by victory, Mao formed the People's Republic of China.

———————— ★ ————————

TWENTY-THREE NUCLEAR TESTS were carried out at Bikini Atoll (a coral reef island) between 1946 and 1958. The original natives were granted $325,000 in compensation and returned to Bikini in 1974. But they were evacuated four years later when new tests showed high levels of residual radioactivity in the region. They sued the United States and were awarded $100 million in compensation.

IN 1952, in the Marshall Islands, the United States conducted tests on a weapon of even greater magnitude. In fact, the hydrogen bomb, or H-bomb, was 500 times more powerful than the atomic bomb dropped on Hiroshima. This thermonuclear device was powered by a fusion reaction rather than the fission reaction of the A-bomb.

IN A SPEECH given in 1946, President Harry Truman introduced the great wartime leader of Great Britain, Winston Churchill. After receiving an honorary degree, Churchill used the term "Iron Curtain" to describe the line in Europe between self-governing nations of Western Europe and those in Eastern Europe under Soviet Communist control.

IN 1957, THE Soviet Union successfully launched the first man-made object placed in orbit, which they called *Sputnik*. This event also fueled fears that the USSR was gaining important ground in the sciences, overtaking the United States.

CONGRESS PASSED the National Defense Education Act in 1958 to enable scholarships and laboratories for science students, who had to sign an oath vowing they had no Communist sympathies.

COMMUNIST FEAR FESTERED within government ranks. In February 1950, Senator Joseph R. McCarthy of Wisconsin charged that the State Department knowingly employed more than 200 Communists. He later revised his claim to a much lower number, and after an investigation, all of his charges were proved to be false.

MCCARTHY, AS CHAIRMAN of the Senate Subcommittee on Governmental Operations, launched investigations of the Voice of America as well as the U.S. Army Signal Corps. J. Edgar Hoover, Federal Bureau of Investigation (FBI) director, assisted McCarthy in hunting Communist spies and sympathizers, often using the power of his bureau.

CONGRESS PASSED the McCarran Internal Security Act in 1950, forcing the registration of all Communist organizations and allowing the government to intern Communists during national emergencies. It also prohibited those people from doing any defense work and prohibited entry into the United States to members of "totalitarian" organizations or governments. The act was passed over President Truman's veto.

MCCARTHY'S BEHAVIOR BECAME known as McCarthyism, meaning any unfounded accusation of subversive activities. Not only were government officials accused and interrogated, but also film directors, military officers, and others from all walks of life were brought before Senate hearings to name those they knew with Communist ties. As a result, many reputations were ruined and careers left in shambles. A few of the accused even committed suicide.

AS WORLD WAR II was raging, the Allied powers had agreed that once Japan was defeated, Korea would become an independent state. After Japan's surrender, General Douglas MacArthur's plan called for the creation of an artificial line at the 38th parallel in Korea. The line essentially split the country in half. The Japanese forces above the parallel surrendered to the Soviet Union, and those to the south to the Americans.

IN JUNE 1950, the Communist government of North Korea launched a full-scale military invasion of neighboring South Korea, a capitalist country. Of course, the Soviet Union was modeling the North Korean government on its own example of Communism.

The United Nations (UN) Security Council voted 9–0 to hold North Korea accountable for the attack. The resolution sent a peacekeeping force, virtually all of which was made up of U.S. troops.

PRESIDENT TRUMAN TERMED the conflict "a police action" and put General MacArthur in command of the UN forces, a post he would hold until his replacement in April 1951. MacArthur held his position on the southeastern portion of the peninsula, and American bombing missions crippled North Korean supply lines. In one of his boldest military operations, General MacArthur planned for a large amphibious landing on the west coast of South Korea at Inchon. Once ashore, American troops would push back the enemy and recapture the capital of Seoul.

AMERICAN FORCES HIT the beaches of Inchon, taking the capital on September 27, 1950. Many thought the war was over with the UN goals having been achieved. The Communists were contained behind the 38th parallel.

SYNGMAN RHEE, PRESIDENT of South Korea, and his troops crossed the 38th parallel and attacked the North Koreans. When they did, President Truman immediately committed UN forces (with the majority of them being U.S. soldiers) to follow Rhee. The next month, Truman and MacArthur met on Wake Island, hoping to discuss the final phase of the Korean War, which they anticipated ending by Thanksgiving.

A LITTLE TOO ARROGANT and confident, MacArthur advanced his men too close to the Chinese border, in violation of his instructions. President Truman's anxiety over MacArthur's actions eventually led to his replacing him with General Matthew Ridgway. General MacArthur faced a Senate hearing for his insubordination to the commander in chief—threatening the Chinese with a powerful U.S.–UN attack without clearing it first with Truman.

GENERAL DWIGHT D. EISENHOWER and his running mate Richard Nixon won the presidential election in 1952. Though peace negotiations had begun in 1951, the new administration inherited the war, and fighting continued for two more years until an armistice was signed on July 27, 1953.

THE AMERICAN PEOPLE liked Ike, the nickname given to Eisenhower as a teenager; he won a war for them with his strategy to storm the beaches of France on D-day.

EISENHOWER KEPT HIS campaign promise to end the Korean conflict. He ran the government much as he ran things in the army, by appointing people to office who would take charge under his supervision. With the United States and Soviet Union as contentious superpowers, President Eisenhower cut back defense spending on traditional weapons while boosting nuclear deterrents.

THE YEAR 1959 brought America two new states. Alaska was admitted as the forty-ninth and most northerly state in January, followed by the volcanic islands in the Pacific—Hawaii—as the fiftieth state in August.

WITH THE AUTOMOBILE freeing Americans to move about the nation, Congress passed the Interstate Highway Act of 1956, making good roads a convenient way of life. People were no longer as isolated, and they certainly knew more about the nation and their neighbors with the influences of radio, television, movie theaters and drive-ins, and the handy 45-rpm vinyl records.

DURING THE 1950s, a very prominent case took center stage, advancing the interests of African Americans. There were laws in seventeen states (mostly Southern) that established racial segregation in public schools. Other states segregated children by district. All justified the practice by using the "separate but equal" standard, according to a Supreme Court decision (Plessy v. Ferguson) in 1896. But in 1954, the NAACP challenged this doctrine at the elementary school level.

THURGOOD MARSHALL AND other NAACP lawyers argued before the Supreme Court that children in all-white schools received a better education than those in all-black schools. It was not an easy decision, but Chief Justice Earl Warren used his considerable influence among the two dissenting justices in order to reach a unanimous decision that May. *Brown v. Board of Education of Topeka, Kansas*, outlawed racial segregation in public schools.

MARSHALL ARGUED THIRTY-TWO cases before the high court, winning twenty-nine of them. In 1967, he became the first African American appointed to the Supreme Court.

IN 1957, PRESIDENT EISENHOWER used federal troops to protect African American students attempting to attend a previously all-white public high school in Little Rock, Arkansas.

ANOTHER LANDMARK MOMENT that propelled civil rights forward involved a weary seamstress named Rosa Parks, who boarded a bus in Montgomery, Alabama, at the end of her workday. Although the forward section was traditionally reserved for white passengers, Parks sat down there. When asked to give up her seat for a white person and move to the back of the bus, she declined. Arrested and jailed, she became a symbol for the struggle to attain racial equality as the African American community rallied around this refined, mild-mannered woman.

★

AFTER ROSA PARKS'S ARREST, local black ministers, led by Dr. Martin Luther King Jr., organized a boycott of the bus system. For over a year, African Americans in Montgomery used carpools, walked to work, or rode horses to get around. Only when the Supreme Court ordered the city to stop segregating black passengers in 1956 did the boycott end.

★

MEMPHIS RECORD PRODUCER Sam Phillips often boasted that with "a white boy who could sing black," he could make a million dollars. In July 1954, Phillips found his ticket to riches and stardom as nineteen-year-old Elvis Presley recorded his first song for Phillips's Sun Records. Singing the rhythm-and-blues style teenagers coveted at the time, Presley was more acceptable to the racially conscious country because he was white. Soon, Presley became known not only as "Elvis the Pelvis," but as the King of Rock 'n' Roll.

★

IN 1951, CLEVELAND, OHIO, disc jockey Alan Freed began playing, among other types, "race music" for a multiracial audience. Freed is credited with coining the phrase "rock 'n' roll" to describe the rhythm and blues music. He also organized the first rock 'n' roll concert, called "The Moondog Coronation Ball" on March 21, 1952.

———————— ★ ————————

FROM 1964 THROUGH 1969, teens listened to a British band called the Beatles. Thirty Beatles songs achieved top-ten status in Billboard magazine charts.

———————— ★ ————————

THE BEATLES, which formed in 1959, was comprised of four musicians born in Liverpool, England. George Harrison and John Lennon played guitar, Paul McCartney was the bassist, and Peter Best (replaced by Ringo Starr in 1962) played drums.

Although their musical style started fresh with early songs such as "I Want to Hold Your Hand," it moved to more innovative and experimental works, culminating in the 1967 release of their album *Sgt. Pepper's Lonely Hearts Club Band.*

———————— ★ ————————

IN 1970, THE Beatles split up to pursue their own musical interests. Speculation about a proposed reunion continued for years until the 1980 murder of John Lennon outside his apartment building, the Dakota, in Manhattan.

———————— ★ ————————

THE BEATLES WERE inducted into the Rock and Roll Hall of Fame in 1988.

———————— ★ ————————

AS AMERICANS APPROACHED the 1960 presidential election, many assumed that since Eisenhower had been a popular president, Vice President Richard Nixon would easily win the 1960 election as the Republican nominee. To beat Nixon, Democrats selected a dashing senator from Massachusetts who was certainly groomed if not destined for the presidency. John F. Kennedy (known by his famous initials, JFK) had a successful and wealthy father (Joseph P. Kennedy, who had served in the New Deal) and maternal grandfather (John F. Fitzgerald, also known as Honey Fitz, who had been the mayor of Boston many years before).

— ★ —

THE MIGRATION OF EAST GERMANS escaping into the West threatened the stability of East Germany. On the night of August 19, 1961, the Berlin Wall was erected as a barricade. President Kennedy commented, "Democracy may not be perfect, but at least we don't have to build walls to keep our people in."

— ★ —

ALTHOUGH KENNEDY HAD the intellect, connections, charm, and World War II heroism (the rescue of his PT-109 crew off the Solomon Islands was well known), he faced certain challenge as the first Irish Catholic to seek executive office. Choosing a Southern running mate—Lyndon B. Johnson of Texas—balanced the Democratic ticket.

— ★ —

KENNEDY BECAME THE first Roman Catholic president of the United States in American history. Every other president before him had been a Protestant Christian.

— ★ —

IN A SERIES of debates, the first ever to be televised, the candidates squared off. Their race remained close, but most agreed that Kennedy seemed much more poised on camera, which emphasized Nixon's haggard appearance. That finesse paid off at the polls, where Kennedy edged ahead in a very narrow defeat of Richard Nixon. In fact, Kennedy garnered 49.7 percent of the popular vote to Nixon's 49.6, though he clearly won the electoral votes needed (303 to Nixon's 219).

AT FORTY-THREE, KENNEDY was the youngest president ever elected (Theodore Roosevelt was slightly younger when he became president, but he had not been elected).

THE SOVIET LAUNCH of Sputnik in the 1950s and cosmonaut Yuri Gagarin's outer space journey in 1961 shifted everyone's attention to mastering space technology before the Russians did. Project Mercury recruited seven brave pilots to become the first astronauts, and soon launched Alan Shepard as the first American in space, followed by John Glenn's 1962 achievement as the first American to orbit Earth.

THE TELSTAR 1 satellite became the first telephone and television satellite as well.

TEST PILOT AND U.S. Air Force officer Chuck Yeager was the first aviator to fly faster than the speed of sound, maneuvering his plane (the *Glamorous Glennis*) through the shock waves produced as the plane neared the speed of Mach 1.

———————— ★ ————————

ON JULY 21, 1969, Neil Armstrong and "Buzz" Aldrin realized Kennedy's dream. Crewman Michael Collins watched as his fellow astronauts landed on and explored the lunar surface. "That's one small step for (a) man, one giant leap for mankind," said Armstrong as he set foot on the moon, to a television audience watching in amazement at this great human achievement.

———————— ★ ————————

TEN MORE ASTRONAUTS explored the moon before the Apollo program ended in 1972.

———————— ★ ————————

IN JANUARY 1959, following a coup on the Caribbean island of Cuba, President Fulgencio Batista fled to the Dominican Republic. For much of the 1950s, he had run a police state that favored the wealthy. Fidel Castro led the Cuban rebels—known as "the bearded ones"—along with his second in command, Ernesto "Che" Guevara. Triumphant, they took Havana, the capital, making Castro the Cuban leader.

———————— ★ ————————

THE UNITED STATES broke diplomatic relations with Cuba in early 1961, and Castro turned to the Soviet Union for assistance. This brought the threat of Communism within ninety miles of U.S. shores, and it was an unsettling factor for both the outgoing Eisenhower and incoming Kennedy administration.

———————— ★ ————————

ON APRIL 19, 1961, approximately 1,500 Cuban exiles returned to the island to mount an invasion they hoped would incite an uprising and topple the Castro regime. Although no U.S. forces were deployed, U.S. support of what became known as the Bay of Pigs incident was undeniable. The CIA had trained antirevolutionary exiles under the Eisenhower administration, and Kennedy approved the invasion. Armed with U.S. weapons, the exiles landed at the Bahía de Cochinos (Bay of Pigs) on Cuba's southern coast. The invasion was not only a failure, but also an embarrassment for the Kennedy administration.

★

IN 1962, U.S. RECONNAISSANCE MISSIONS flying over Cuba photographed Soviet-managed construction work and spotted a ballistic missile in October 1962. Castro, certain that the United States would try another invasion, had agreed to Soviet missiles for his island's protection.

★

FOR SEVERAL TENSE DAYS during the Cuban missile crisis, Kennedy and Soviet Premier Nikita Khrushchev communicated through diplomatic channels. The world held its breath for fear of nuclear war between the superpowers. The crisis was solved after the Soviets agreed to remove the missiles and allow U.S. onsite inspection in return for the guarantee not to invade the island nation. Kennedy accepted, agreed to remove U.S. missiles from Turkey, and suspended the blockade, but Cuba refused to permit the promised inspection, out of anger at Soviet submission. Aerial photography did reveal that the missile bases were being dismantled.

★

PRESIDENT KENNEDY'S FAMOUS SPEECH in Berlin during the summer of 1962 contained the German phrase: *"Ich bin ein Berliner."* Because President Kennedy did not speak German, he trusted his aides to translate the English phrase "I am a Berliner" into German. However, they didn't get the wording quite right. In German, the word *ein* does not exactly translate as "a(n)." In German, when a person is talking about himself he would say, *"Ich bein Berliner."* Because President Kennedy put the *"ein"* in the sentence, he was not saying that he was a "citizen of Berlin" but that he was a kind of jelly donut called a "Berliner."

———————— ★ ————————

ON NOVEMBER 22, 1963, Mrs. Kennedy, the vice president, and Mrs. Johnson, along with Governor John B. Connally of Texas and his wife, accompanied President Kennedy on a visit to Dallas, Texas. En route to a downtown luncheon, the president chose to ride in an open convertible through the motorcade route with his wife sitting beside him. As the motorcade approached an underpass, Kennedy was shot in the head. Rushed to Parkland Hospital, the president never regained consciousness.

———————— ★ ————————

GOVERNOR CONNALLY HAD also been shot, but survived surgery, and Vice President Lyndon Johnson, who had ridden two cars behind in the motorcade, was sworn in as president before the entourage flew back to Washington that day.

———————— ★ ————————

HOURS LATER AFTER the Kennedy shooting, Dallas police arrested the suspect Lee Harvey Oswald, an employee in a warehouse building along the motorcade route, who was also charged with shooting a police officer the same afternoon. Oswald's background check quickly revealed he'd suffered a troubled youth, defected to the Soviet Union (where he was denied citizenship), and had obvious Communist leanings.

———————— ★ ————————

OSWALD WAS HIMSELF ASSASSINATED while being transferred from one jail to another. Dallas nightclub owner Jack Ruby sprang from a group of reporters to shoot the suspect, who also died at Parkland Hospital.

———————— ★ ————————

FOLLOWING THE PRESIDENT'S DEATH and cognizant of his quest for space exploration, NASA renamed its space center on a promontory in eastern Florida, known as Cape Canaveral, the John F. Kennedy Space Center. Today, visitors can watch satellite and space flight launches, view an IMAX presentation, take tours, and learn about America's space program.

———————— ★ ————————

ON NOVEMBER 24, 1963, the nation mourned as the president's body was carried by horse-drawn carriage from the White House to the Rotunda of the Capitol. Hundreds of thousands filed past the coffin to pay their respects. A state funeral took place the next day. Foreign dignitaries and heads of state attended. Citizens lined the streets of Washington, DC, as the funeral cortege made its way to Arlington National Cemetery.

———————— ★ ————————

FREEDOM RIDES ACROSS THE SOUTH were common in the decades-old struggle for civil rights in a segregated society. James Meredith made headlines when he tried to enroll in the all-white University of Mississippi and the governor personally blocked his attempts despite federal law. This being the early 1960s, President Kennedy had sent in federal marshals. Governor George Wallace of Alabama blocked the University of Alabama, and once again, Kennedy sent in the National Guard.

———————— ★ ————————

MALCOLM X, ASSASSINATED IN 1965, gave voice to the Black Power movement, urging blacks to reject white culture in favor of their own heritage. Although at first he preached violence as a means of expression, he later devoted himself to peace. The Black Panther activists also staged antiwar protests and stood for the black cause.

THE MOST NOTED of the leaders during the Civil Rights movement was the Reverend Martin Luther King Jr., who had organized the bus boycotts during Rosa Parks's struggle in the 1950s. As a clergyman, he used his vision of nonviolent confrontation to challenge segregation and the racial divide, and in doing so, he convinced other Americans to join his cause.

★

KING, ALONG WITH other black leaders, organized the August 1963 March on Washington. During this march he delivered his famous "I Have a Dream" speech. King's speech showed not only his articulate and passionate delivery, but also his moral character, and it gave momentum to his followers and their cause. As a result of his work, he was awarded the Nobel Peace Prize in 1964.

★

CONTINUING HIS WORK to speak out for equality, King made another speech in Memphis, Tennessee, on April 3, 1968, where he said, "We've got some difficult days ahead, but it really doesn't matter to me now, because I've been to the mountaintop." The next evening, on April 4, an assassin gunned down Martin Luther King Jr. as he stood on the balcony of his Memphis motel.

★

PRESIDENTS' DAY IS celebrated in February to honor two presidents, Abraham Lincoln and George Washington. The holiday is celebrated in the

United States on the third Monday in February. Since Presidents' Day in 1971, two other national holidays were named to honor individuals: Columbus Day and Martin Luther King's birthday.

★

BY 1884, FRANCE had annexed Vietnam, placing it under colonial rule. In 1921, however, the revolutionary Ho Chi Minh created a nationalist party seeking independence from France. During World War II, the Japanese wrested control temporarily from the French, and as Japanese forces surrendered, Ho Chi Minh launched a full-scale revolt, taking Hanoi, the capital.

★

FRANCE REFUSED TO allow the independence movement, and by 1946 re-established rule, fearing (along with the United States) that all of Asia could become Communist as China fell to Mao Tse-tung. President Truman sent military supplies and funds for the French war in Vietnam, aiming to stem Communist imperialism.

★

A CEASE-FIRE IN JULY 1954 established a buffer zone between North and South Vietnam. The Communists, led by Ho Chi Minh, controlled the North, while Ngo Dinh Diem stepped in as interim premier in the south.

★

SOUTH KOREA SENT military advisors and aid to assist South Vietnam. Diem's regime, however, was corrupt, complicating matters for the United States as Vietcong Communists within South Vietnam killed Diem's authorities. General Maxwell Taylor, one of Kennedy's top advisors, suggested that sending a few thousand soldiers would quickly take care of the situation, and Vice President Johnson concurred. Kennedy withdrew support of Diem's regime. Shortly thereafter, the Vietnamese overthrew Diem, who was later murdered.

———————— ★ ————————

PRESIDENT JOHNSON WAS wary of committing U.S. forces, but when North Vietnamese torpedo boats allegedly attacked U.S. naval destroyers in the Gulf of Tonkin, Johnson ordered immediate retaliation. Later investigation cast doubt on whether the North Vietnamese really attacked or whether radar blips confused naval personnel. But this occurred only after Congress passed the Gulf of Tonkin Resolution, authorizing Johnson to wage war in Indochina with whatever force he desired. By the end of 1964, approximately 20,000 troops had already been sent to the region.

———————— ★ ————————

THE UNITED STATES began a bombing campaign, code-named Operation Rolling Thunder, to stem the stream of supplies from Communist North Vietnam. The operation met with little success. Missions were halted and then stepped up against Hanoi and Haiphong. Relentless aid streamed in to North Vietnam from the Soviet Union and China.

———————— ★ ————————

IN 1965, WHEN it became clear that mere bombing wasn't enough, the United States sent ground combat troops to Vietnam. Helicopter-borne troops surprised villages harboring suspected Communist supporters. Troops often destroyed such villages, forcing the Vietnamese to find new homes. Fighting became more brutal, as the Vietcong and the North Vietnamese were experts at mine warfare.

———————— ★ ————————

THOUGH THE SOUTH VIETNAMESE elected a new president, the conflict dragged on. In 1968, U.S. troops massacred Vietnamese civilians at My Lai in the aftermath of the Tet offensive in Saigon (where Vietcong soldiers attacked the U.S. embassy as well as multiple military targets throughout all of Vietnam).

WAR PROTESTS DURING the 1968 Democratic National Convention in Chicago provoked riot police. The objections to the war were so profound that they convinced President Lyndon Johnson not to seek re-election in 1968.

———— ★ ————

IN 1970, DURING a demonstration against the Vietnam War at Kent State University in Ohio, National Guardsmen fired into a crowd of unarmed students, killing four and wounding eleven.

———— ★ ————

VISITORS TO WASHINGTON, DC, can visit the Vietnam Memorial, also known as "the Wall." The walls of the memorial are deep-black granite and form a V, deepest in the earth at the vertex, tapering and rising to ground level over their length of nearly 500 feet. The Wall is a moving tribute to Vietnam veterans, listing the names of 58,249 Americans who perished in the war.

———— ★ ————

PEACE NEGOTIATIONS OPENED in Paris in May 1968, and after Nixon won election, he began a gradual withdrawal of forces, which had reached a high of 550,000. South Vietnamese forces with U.S. helicopter support attacked Communist bases in Cambodia in 1970. Nixon continued to withdraw troops while the conflict lingered. Congress withdrew the Gulf of Tonkin Resolution on December 31, 1970, and peace came in 1973.

———— ★ ————

SOUTH VIETNAM'S PRESIDENT announced an unconditional surrender in April 1975.

★

LYNDON JOHNSON DECLARED a war on poverty and introduced extensive social legislation, vowing shortly after Kennedy's death that equal rights for Americans needed to become law. The legislation was passed quickly, but turmoil took its toll despite its passage. Race riots flared up in many cities, such as the Watts Riots in Los Angeles. Protests regarding the Vietnam War also escalated to the point that Johnson refused to seek a presidential nomination.

★

WITH JOHNSON OUT of the running, Robert F. Kennedy, who had left his post as attorney general to become a senator representing the state of New York, sought the Democratic nomination. Kennedy was a champion of the downtrodden, particularly concerned about problems in urban ghettos and Appalachia.

★

AFTER WINNING THE essential California primary, Kennedy gave his victory speech and exited through a hotel kitchen, where a Jordanian immigrant named Sirhan Sirhan waited with a gun. Severely wounded, Kennedy died in a Los Angeles hospital the next day, June 6, 1968. His funeral service was held in New York City's Saint Patrick's Cathedral, and he is buried not far from the grave of his brother at Arlington National Cemetery.

★

VICE PRESIDENT HUBERT HUMPHREY won the nomination that summer and was set to run against Richard Nixon, once vice president in the Eisenhower administration. Having been defeated for the high office in 1960, Nixon, who had once pledged to the media that they wouldn't have him to kick around again, returned to politics, vowing to end the Vietnam War. Meanwhile, Governor George Wallace of Alabama mounted a third-party campaign. Nixon, who had named Governor Spiro T. Agnew of Maryland as his running mate, gained a comfortable majority of the electoral votes (though he won by a slim margin of the popular vote).

THE BIRTH CONTROL PILL, which was introduced in 1960, gained popularity as well, leading to a sexual revolution and a change in lifestyle for many. By 1973, about 10 million women were using "the pill."

SOME OF THOSE who dropped out of traditional society during the 1960s were called "hippies," and they gravitated to areas such as the Haight-Ashbury section of San Francisco. They became known as "flower children" because they believed that utopia was found in nature.

THE SUMMER OF LOVE refers to the summer of 1967, when thousands of young people traveled to San Francisco from all over the world and the hippie counterculture movement came into public awareness. The Human Be-In (modeled on the sit-in) in San Francisco's Golden Gate Park is said to have started the Summer of Love.

IN AUGUST OF 1969, more than 300,000 young people gathered at Max Yasgur's dairy farm in the small Catskills town of Bethel, New York, for the Woodstock Music and Art Fair.

AMERICANS WERE NOW influenced by people like Abby Hoffman and Jerry Rubin and musicians such as the Beatles, who were disciples of transcendental meditation (Eastern religions caught on in force during the decade). After John Lennon married Yoko Ono, the unconventional pair decided to host a "bed-in for peace" for their honeymoon. They stayed in the presidential suite of a large Amsterdam hotel for seven days, protesting the war.

BERRY GORDY, an African American who made Motown Records of Detroit, Michigan, the most profitable minority business of its time, also built the fortunes and fame of artists such as Stevie Wonder, the Temptations, the Four Tops, Smokey Robinson and the Miracles, and Diana Ross and the Supremes. Their achievements helped break down the racial divide in America.

AS THE 1960s CONTINUED, folk music carried with it songs of protest with a sense of growing militancy against the war in Vietnam. Peter, Paul, and Mary; Joan Baez; and Bob Dylan caught on with their music and their message. But there was also more traditional music.

IN 1966, *The Sound of Music* won an Academy Award for best film, which starred Julie Andrews, fresh from her recent success with *Mary Poppins.*

IN THE 1960s, being fashionable meant wearing false eyelashes, Vidal Sassoon hairstyles, and miniskirts, as the rail-thin model Twiggy displayed so well. Knee- or thigh-high boots completed the fashion ensemble.

TELEVISION CAPTURED AMERICA'S ATTENTION in the 1960s, turning the world into a virtual global village. Soap manufacturing companies began to sponsor dramatic television series that became known as "soap operas." Sporting events were increasingly broadcast, and cartoons appeared on the television as well.

---------------- ★ ----------------

COMEDIES AND TALK SHOWS aired at night, and the networks broadcast events such as the landing on the moon. Space exploration of the fictional variety could be seen with the starship *Enterprise*, as the show *Star Trek* launched in 1966 with characters Captain James Kirk and Mr. Spock.

---------------- ★ ----------------

WHEN FRED ROGERS began working at NBC in the 1950s, he knew there had to be a way to make a difference using this new medium. So when educational television began in his home area of Pittsburgh, Pennsylvania, Rogers left a promising career to begin his life's work. *Mister Rogers' Neighborhood* began airing in the United States in 1968.

---------------- ★ ----------------

IN 1969, *Sesame Street*, funded by the Children's Television Workshop, began as an hour for preschool children in deprived areas. It quickly took hold with characters such as Big Bird, Cookie Monster, and Kermit the Frog, helping children everywhere learn their letters, numbers, and social skills.

---------------- ★ ----------------

NIXON'S INITIATIVES IN FOREIGN AFFAIRS dated back to the Eisenhower administration. As vice president, while escorting Soviet Premier Nikita Khrushchev through a model U.S. kitchen, he debated the merits of the two countries' political systems in what was termed the "kitchen debate."

ON OCTOBER 25, 1971, the General Assembly of the United Nations withdrew their recognition of the Republic of China (Taiwan) as the legitimate government of China, instead recognizing the People's Republic of China as the legitimate government. On November 15, 1971, the People's Republic of China made its formal entry into the United Nations.

★

NIXON WAS THE first president to meet with Communist leaders in Moscow and Beijing, signing trade agreements with both countries and a treaty with the USSR to limit the deployment of antiballistic missile systems. His secretary of state, Henry Kissinger, was an especially skilled diplomat, helping to establish strategic détente with both the Soviet Union and China.

★

NIXON WAS OUTRAGED when Daniel Ellsberg, a former serviceman turned civilian, compiled a compendium of material that came to be known as "the Pentagon Papers." The papers were related to the Vietnam War, essentially disclosing that the war's objectives were not achieved and that the United States had planned to oust another country's head of state. Ellsberg contacted the *New York Times*, and the papers began to be published. Nixon sought an injunction to prevent the publication, but the Supreme Court held in a 6-to-3 decision (*New York Times Co. v. U.S.*) that the injunctions were unconstitutional prior restraints and therefore a violation of the First Amendment's protection of a free press.

★

IT WAS ALSO revealed that a White House team had placed illegal wiretaps on Ellsberg's telephone and had broken into his psychiatrist's office in an attempt to discredit him.

IN THE ELECTION OF 1972, Richard Nixon won easily over his Democratic opponent, Senator George McGovern of South Dakota. Later it came out that White House operatives had dug up information regarding McGovern's first vice-presidential pick, making out Thomas Eagleton to be mentally ill. McGovern replaced Eagleton on the ticket with Sargent Shriver, a Kennedy in-law and the first director of the Peace Corps.

VICE PRESIDENT SPIRO AGNEW resigned in October 1973 after his financial misconduct was revealed. The vice president had allegedly accepted $29,500 in bribes during his tenure as governor of Maryland. President Nixon nominated Gerald R. Ford, a Michigan congressman, to succeed Agnew as vice president.

IN 1972 THE MUNICH OLYMPIC GAMES were marked by extraordinary accomplishments and unbelievable tragedy. Mark Spitz, a twenty-two-year-old American swimmer, won a record seven gold medals. In an act of terrorism by Black September, an Arab terrorist group, eleven Israeli Olympians were murdered, two at the Olympic Village and nine at the Munich Airport.

NIXON'S POPULARITY SUFFERED when the economy endured severe inflation, due in some measure to a U.S.–USSR agreement under which the Soviet Union could purchase huge quantities of grain. This devalued the U.S. dollar again. Nixon then cut government funding to many social programs in order to be more fiscally conservative, but this further strained relations with Congress.

THE FIVE MEN arrested breaking into the Democratic National Committee (DNC) offices at Watergate apartment and office complex in Washington, DC, included Charles Colson, G. Gordon Liddy, and Howard Hunt Jr. Collectively, the group was known as "the White House plumbers," given the name for their ability to plug White House information leaks. As history would record, however, their duties extended to spying and other odd jobs.

★

"THE WHITE HOUSE plumbers" were arrested after a piece of tape left over a door lock tipped off security.

★

THE DNC OFFICE break-in targeted the Democratic Party leader Larry O'Brien, who had connections dating back to the 1960 election that Nixon had lost to Kennedy.

★

THE TWO *WASHINGTON POST* **JOURNALISTS** assigned to cover the break-in—dubbed a "third-rate burglary" by the White House—were Bob Woodward and Carl Bernstein. As they gathered clues, the two pieced together a trail of money and cover-ups that led back to the Committee to Re-elect the President (CREEP) and to the Oval Office. U.S. District Court Judge John Sirica remained persistent in his questioning, which also helped crack the case. During the 1973 trial, they learned that this group had attempted to steal documents and had placed wiretaps on telephones.

★

FOR NEARLY THIRTY-THREE YEARS, the identity of the main source for Woodward and Bernstein was keep secret and known only as "Deep Throat." William Mark Felt Sr., a retired agent of the United States Federal Bureau of Investigation, who retired in 1973 as the Bureau's number two official, revealed himself on May 31, 2005, to be the Watergate scandal whistleblower called "Deep Throat."

A SENATE COMMITTEE on the Watergate scandal convened, as did an investigation by special prosecutor Archibald Cox. This investigation truly shed light on the espionage conducted against Nixon's political rivals. With each revelation, it seemed as if one more official in the Nixon administration was forced out or resigned. The president's own counsel, John Dean, testified that there was a cancer on the presidency.

WHEN IT WAS disclosed that the president routinely taped Oval Office conversations, investigators had the tool they needed to chip away at the deception and reveal the truth. Yet President Nixon, claiming executive privilege, refused to hand over the tapes. He viewed them as his personal property.

WHEN NIXON FINALLY surrendered his tapes, they were extensively edited versions, one with an eighteen-and-a-half-minute gap. In the end, Nixon only bought himself some time as pressure mounted to release the tapes in unaltered form.

THE PRESIDENT SAW many resignations of key advisors and staff. When Nixon ordered the firing of special investigator Cox over the tape matter, he saw yet another of his attorneys general leave the administration. The greatest exodus of staff became known as the Saturday Night Massacre. It outraged the public and diminished everyone's trust in the president.

IN OCTOBER 1973, the House Judiciary Committee began considering impeachment proceedings against Nixon, who was stalling with subpoenaed material. The appointment of yet another special investigator, this time Leon Jaworski, did little to quell the outcry. On July 24, 1974, the U.S. Supreme Court ruled in an appeal, *United States v. Nixon*, that the president could not use his claim of executive privilege in refusing to hand over the tapes.

THE HOUSE VOTED to introduce three impeachment articles that same month with the charges of obstructing justice, abusing presidential power, and refusing to obey subpoenas by the House of Representatives.

ON AUGUST 5, bowing to pressure, Nixon released tapes that clearly showed his involvement in the Watergate cover-up as early as June 1972. The tape that did the most damage, recorded on June 23, became known as "the smoking gun," for the president could be heard discussing payoffs and other illegal actions.

AFTER A VISIT from Republican leader Barry Goldwater and others, Nixon announced that he would resign from office. On August 9, 1974, he flew away from the White House in a helicopter, and shortly thereafter, Vice

President Gerald R. Ford was sworn in as president, inheriting a nation in shock and dismay at the problems in their government. He was the first vice president and the first president to ascend to both positions without being elected to those offices.

★

IN SEPTEMBER 1974, President Ford issued a pardon to Nixon for all federal crimes he may have committed during his administration. It was an unpopular decision and may have cost Ford re-election in 1976. Yet it spared the nation a great deal of lingering turmoil.

★

ALMOST EVERYONE ASSOCIATED with Watergate went on to pen memoirs or accounts of the political saga, including John Dean with his book *Blind Ambition*. In his retirement, former president Richard Nixon wrote books on political affairs, including *No More Vietnams* (1985), *In the Arena* (1990), and *Beyond Peace* (1994).

★

NIXON DIED OF a stroke in 1994 and was buried next to his wife, Pat, on the grounds of his presidential library.

★

SOME WOULD SAY that Gerald Ford's presidency existed in the shadows of disadvantage. He was never elected, even as a vice-presidential candidate. Though he'd served twenty-five years in the House of Representatives, he was barely known on the national scene.

★

WHEN HE WAS BORN, future president Gerald R. Ford was not named "Gerald R. Ford," he was named after his birth father, Leslie Lynch King. When his mother married Gerald R. Ford in Michigan in 1916, Ford adopted her three-year-old son as well. The couple renamed the boy after his adoptive father, Gerald Rudolph Ford, Jr.

IN THE 1970s, quasi-religions and cults became popular, sometimes with tragic outcomes. In 1978, Jim Jones convinced followers to move to Guyana and commit mass suicide. More than 900 members of the People's Temple perished after consuming a grape drink mixed with cyanide and Valium.

JIM JONES'S MASS SUICIDE REHEARSALS called White Nights were actually not voluntary but forced. According to one survivor, people who refused to commit suicide were held down and shot with needles filled with potassium cyanide. They even went around with stethoscopes to see if they still had a heartbeat, and if they did, they'd shoot that person.

WHEN NEW YORK CITY almost went bankrupt, it turned to Washington for help. At first Ford denied the request, but pressure mounted from other states feeling the fallout of New York's troubled economy. The cumulative effects of all these factors made it possible for another virtual unknown to hit the political circuit in 1976—Jimmy Carter.

JIMMY CARTER, with his genuine, toothy smile, was a peanut farmer and former navy man who had studied nuclear physics. When he ran against incumbent Gerald Ford, he won the 1976 presidential election.

JIMMY CARTER WAS the thirty-ninth president of the United States, but he was first president in one way at least: President Carter is the first president of the United States to be born in a hospital.

CARTER'S BIGGEST OBSTACLE in turning around the economy became the energy crisis. Crude oil prices had continued to rise, leading to a shortage of gasoline, rationing, and long lines at the pumps.

ONE AREA IN which Carter certainly excelled was hosting President el-Sadat of Egypt and Prime Minister Begin of Israel in talks at Camp David, the presidential retreat in Maryland, for Mideast peace accords. A state of war had existed between the two nations from 1948 to 1978 when Carter intervened.

YEARS BEFORE, THE CIA had used covert aid to help restore Muhammad Reza Pahlavi as the shah of Iran in order to protect its interest in this volatile region. But the shah's regime lost its religious roots and became corrupt and autocratic. Conservative Muslims led by the Ayatollah Ruhollah Khomeini opposed the Iranian government, inciting a revolution that deposed the shah and sent him and his family into exile. When the shah sought asylum in the United States, the ayatollah demanded his return, along with the billions of dollars the shah had allegedly hidden abroad.

ON NOVEMBER 4, 1979, a mob of Islamic students attacked the U.S. embassy in Tehran, taking sixty-six members of the staff as hostages. Though thirteen were soon released, the other fifty-three remained hostages for 444

days. Negotiations did not secure their return, nor did a failed U.S. commando raid the following April. Carter ordered an airborne rescue attempt in April 1980 that failed miserably. On day 445 of the Iranian hostage crisis, the hostages were released, but only as Jimmy Carter's presidency ended at noon that day.

DURING THE LATE 1960s, abortion became the topic of debate in the political arena. "Pro-choice" advocates believed that only a woman and her doctor should decide whether to end a pregnancy. They argued that life begins when the fetus can survive on its own outside the mother's womb. "Pro-life" advocates argued that life begins at conception and that states should prohibit the procedure. Many women had illegal abortions, risking their health and their lives.

IN 1973, THE U.S. Supreme Court ruled in the case of *Roe v. Wade* that the state cannot restrict a woman's right to an abortion during the first trimester, that the state can regulate the abortion procedure during the second trimester "in ways that are reasonably related to maternal health," and that in the third trimester, a state can choose to restrict or even to proscribe abortion as it sees fit.

GLORIA STEINEM, a writer and political activist, founded the magazine *Ms.* in 1971 when women's magazines began covering crucial topics such as health and sexuality, law, work, and the arts. Women everywhere began insisting on the title "Ms." as opposed to "Miss" or "Mrs.," asserting that the courtesy title of their male counterparts (Mr.) did not reveal their marital status.

BY AUGUST 1974, the Equal Rights Amendment had been ratified by thirty-three of the required thirty-eight states. A congressional mandate had set March 1979 as the deadline for ratification, and by June 1978, only three additional states had approved the ERA. Even when given an extension for approval, the amendment failed to be ratified.

THE 1970s SAW an increase in all kinds of activism. Gay liberation occurred all over the country, but particularly in areas such as New York's Greenwich Village and San Francisco. In 1973, the American Psychiatric Association issued a position statement that held that homosexuality was no longer to be considered a mental illness or psychiatric disorder.

RALPH NADER BROUGHT consumerism to the forefront, making him an instant enemy of corporate America, whose products he questioned. There is little doubt that Nader's efforts raised the quality of goods. In 1965, Nader's book *Unsafe at Any Speed* exposed corruption in the automobile industry, in particular the ability to make cars far safer and the hesitancy to do so.

IN 1979, THE public's concern for the environment grew when an accident occurred at Three Mile Island, the site of a pressurized-water nuclear reactor outside Harrisburg, Pennsylvania. A maintenance error and a defective valve led to the loss of coolant. The safety systems seemed to have worked properly but when the emergency cooling system was shut off, a partial core meltdown (with resulting damage) occurred, and a small amount of radioactive gas escaped from the containment building. The financial cost to the utility was substantial, but the public scare was even worse.

BECAUSE OF the incident at Three Mile Island, legislation was soon enacted requiring the Nuclear Regulatory Commission to adopt far more stringent standards for the design and construction of nuclear power plants, as well as preparation of emergency plans to protect public health and the environment. Several nuclear power plants already under construction were canceled.

———————— ★ ————————

IN 1974, HENRY LOUIS "HANK" AARON hit his 715th home run, breaking Babe Ruth's record that had stood for thirty-nine years. He was one of the first black players to enter major league baseball.

———————— ★ ————————

MUHAMMAD ALI FIRST came on the scene in the 1960s as Cassius M. Clay Jr., an Olympic gold medalist and later world heavyweight champ, but he was stripped of the title when convicted of draft evasion. He took a new name when he joined a Black Muslim sect, and won a Supreme Court reversal. He regained the heavyweight crown in 1974 against George Foreman.

———————— ★ ————————

THE FIRST BLACK MAN to win a major tennis tournament, Arthur Ashe Jr. began playing the game in the segregated parks of Richmond, Virginia. He won important tennis titles, survived heart surgery, and retired from the game. Later, he developed HIV, likely acquired through blood transfusions. He became an active fundraiser prior to his death.

———————— ★ ————————

WINNER OF THE LADIES' FIGURE SKATING GOLD MEDAL at the 1976 Winter Olympics, Dorothy Hamill not only gained international popularity but brought a resurgence to figure skating, her own trademark "Hamill Camel" to her spins, and a new hairstyle that was all the rage in America.

IN WHAT WAS dubbed the "Battle of the Sexes," the tennis star Billie Jean King defeated her male opponent Bobby Riggs in three straight sets. King was one of the most successful tennis players in the history of Wimbledon.

BRUCE JENNER WON the Olympic decathlon event at the 1976 Olympic Games in Montreal, and was one of the first athletes to use his Olympic popularity as a springboard to wealth and celebrity off the track.

AS THE PREMIER pro golfer of the 1960s and 1970s, Jack Nicklaus consistently captured major pro tournaments, including the U.S. Open, Masters, and Professional Golfers' Association (PGA) Championship.

THE AMERICAN SWIMMER Mark Spitz won seven gold medals at the 1972 Olympic Games in Munich, West Germany. He set world records in many races, including the 200-meter butterfly event.

DURING THE 1970s, the Pittsburgh Steelers was the first NFL team to win four Super Bowls. Head coach Chuck Noll led the talented quarterback Terry Bradshaw, defensive end "Mean" Joe Greene, running back Franco Harris, and linebackers Jack Ham and Jack Lambert.

THE END OF THE MILLENNIUM AND THE START OF A NEW CENTURY

In the 1980s, *the nation seemed to be searching for old-fashioned values in their leaders as well as new discoveries they could have never imagined, which would open up a world of possibilities for both themselves and their nation. With the good came the bad though, and the final eight years of the twentieth century included terrorist strikes on New York City and Washington, a booming economy with falling deficits, a two-term Democrat as president with a Republican Congress from 1995–2000, and the second impeachment in United States history.*

The beginning of the millennium held its fair share of bumps along the road as well, but offered a promising look at the future with a new focus on technology, the environment, and civil rights. This chapter explores our recent history and the events, people, and laws that bring us up to the beginning of the new millennium.

AS THE CARTER ADMINISTRATION failed to revive a sagging economy, Americans looked to Reagan for leadership. Reagan blasted Carter on the campaign trail on everything from the struggling economy to the need for a strong military. Failure to resolve the Iranian hostage crisis contributed to Ronald Reagan's defeat of Carter in the presidential election in 1980.

REAGAN HAD PREVIOUSLY tried to enter the national political arena, challenging Gerald Ford for the Republican nomination in 1976. During this campaign, he briefly considered former president Ford as a potential running mate, but selected George Bush instead.

ON JANUARY 20, 1981, the day of President Reagan's inauguration, the United States released almost $8 billion in Iranian assets and the hostages were freed after 444 days in Iranian detention.

PRESIDENT REAGAN SET the record for being the oldest president ever to hold office. He was almost seventy-eight when he left office in 1989. The previous record holder, Andrew Jackson, was sixty-nine when he left office in 1837. Within a few months of starting his term Reagan passed Jackson and turned seventy during his first year in office.

ON DECEMBER 8, 1980, John Lennon was shot to death by a deranged fan outside his Manhattan apartment building. After returning home from a recording session with his wife, Yoko Ono, Lennon stepped from his limousine and was shot twice by Mark David Chapman. A section of Central Park was named Strawberry Fields in honor of John Lennon in 1981.

———————— ★ ————————

ON MARCH 31, 1981, Reagan's presidency was almost cut short by an assassination attempt. His attacker, John W. Hinckley, was an unstable drifter acting out a fantasy to gain the attention of actress Jodie Foster. Foster had starred in the movie *Taxi Driver*, which partly dealt with political assassination. Hinckley was found not guilty by reason of insanity and committed to a mental hospital. Reagan recovered from the shooting.

———————— ★ ————————

IN OCTOBER 1987, Wall Street investors panicked, causing stocks to plummet 508 points, even more sharply than they'd done in 1929. However, the nation did not slump into a depression, but recovered from "Black Monday."

———————— ★ ————————

PRESIDENT REAGAN APPOINTED three new justices to the Supreme Court, including Sandra Day O'Connor, the first woman to serve on the high bench.

———————— ★ ————————

KNOWN AS THE "TEFLON PRESIDENT" because none of his mistakes seemed to stick, Reagan won re-election in 1984 against his Democratic opponent, Walter Mondale, who had named Geraldine Ferraro as his vice-presidential running mate—the first woman to run for this office. Democrats slowly gained control in Congress, which made legislative initiatives difficult for President Reagan as his tenure neared an end.

———————— ★ ————————

THE MILITARY BOASTED of its Strategic Defense Initiative technology, often called "Star Wars," which was supposed to permit the United States to intercept enemy missiles before they hit their targets. Reagan had insisted on the technology, though many felt it was too expensive. Some called it a hoax to make the Soviets believe the United States had a strategic advantage.

BECAUSE THE UNITED STATES and the Soviet Union were struggling for world domination and didn't want to use their nuclear weapons, their confrontation was called a "cold" war because there was no actual fighting. The tactics involved included the Eisenhower Doctrine, which stated that the United States would help any country that was against Communism and would use any means, including nuclear weapons, if the Unites States or one of its allies was threatened. This policy was called *containment*, and it worked for over fifty years until the fall of the Soviet Union in the 1990s.

THE COMMUNIST EMPIRE, as generations had known it and feared it, unexpectedly began to unravel during the tenure of Mikhail Gorbachev. He initiated a campaign called perestroika (Russian for "restructuring"), reforming and revitalizing the Soviet system that had been in place for decades. Under the new Soviet system, prices soared, as did unemployment. When people could get to the stores through the long lines, they often found nothing of value. Unable to navigate the change as the Soviet economy continued its decline, Gorbachev watched as the USSR collapsed in 1991.

AS THE IRON CURTAIN COLLAPSED, one image captured the moment—the toppling of the Berlin Wall. An East German government statement broadcast on November 9, 1989, stated that the crossing of the border would be permitted. As East Germans crossed into West Germany, the first step of German reunification began. The Wall was subsequently destroyed over a period of several weeks.

REAGAN'S ADMINISTRATION BECAME embroiled in controversy, damaging his reputation as an honest communicator. In November 1986, word leaked to newspapers that the United States had secretly sold weapons to Iran, diverting approximately $30 million in profits from these sales to help the Contras fight the leftist Sandinista government in Nicaragua. The investigative committee found no evidence that President Reagan had broken the law, but admitted that Reagan may have known about or participated in a cover-up of the scandal.

---- ★ ----

THE IRAN-CONTRA AFFAIR had weakened his political clout, and Congress openly rejected some of Reagan's initiatives. Congress overrode a presidential veto of a civil-rights enforcement bill and refused funding for the Contras' military operations.

---- ★ ----

IT HAD BEEN alleged that there were ties between the Contras and drug smugglers—this in an era where the first lady had publicly espoused a campaign for school children called "Just Say No" to drugs.

---- ★ ----

TOWARD THE END of Reagan's tenure as president, it was reported that he dozed off during cabinet meetings and spent less and less time on presidential duties.

---- ★ ----

ON JULY 13, 1985, over 160,000 supporters gathered in Philadelphia and London to watch Live Aid, a rock concert aimed at raising funds for famine relief in Ethiopia. Performers included Mick Jagger, Tina Turner, Queen, Phil

Collins, Bob Dylan, Paul McCartney, Sting, Madonna, and U2, among others. It was one of the largest television broadcasts of all time: an estimated 1.5 billion viewers, across 100 countries, watched the live broadcast.

———————— ★ ————————

PRESIDENT GEORGE HERBERT WALKER BUSH won the election of 1988 against Democratic rival Michael Dukakis, the governor of Massachusetts. Bush came across as a more patriotic campaigner than his rival, and though he took some flak for his choice of Senator Dan Quayle as running mate (against Senator Lloyd Bentsen), he triumphed. Many did not see Quayle as presidential, and he became fodder for late-night comedians, further eroding public confidence.

———————— ★ ————————

GEORGE BUSH BELIEVED that the former Soviet Union could become an ally, and that if the Cold War ended, American taxpayers would no longer have to finance the military might it had necessitated. Thus, Bush helped edge the Soviet leader toward democracy and gravitated toward foreign affairs rather than many domestic initiatives.

———————— ★ ————————

IN 1992, MANUEL NORIEGA, an agent of the Central Intelligence Agency (CIA) while President Bush had been the agency's director, was convicted on drug and racketeering charges. Bush sent troops to Panama to assist in a coup against Noriega. The invasion lasted only days and resulted in Noriega's capture and return to the mainland.

———————— ★ ————————

IRAQI LEADER SADDAM HUSSEIN launched an offensive on neighboring Kuwait in August 1990. The tiny nation, governed by a sheik, held

10 percent of the world's oil reserves. President Bush mounted an unprecedented global alliance against the Iraqi assault, trying to protect the largely defenseless nation, but also to prevent future Iraqi conquests, since Saudi Arabia bordered Saddam's forces and was home to another 25 percent of the world's reserves.

★

BUSH LIKENED HUSSEIN TO HITLER and created a coalition under the auspices of the United Nations. Bush convinced the Saudi Arabians to allow a U.S. troop presence on their soil, and the U.S. Department of Defense deployed military weapons and soldiers in the largest such undertaking since Vietnam. Despite Hussein's requests for a portion of Kuwait, Bush held firm to his demand for complete withdrawal and warned of the consequences if he was not heeded. The proverbial line in the sand was drawn with a deadline of January 15 for Hussein's withdrawal.

★

THE UNITED NATIONS SECURITY COUNCIL had already sanctioned the use of force, if necessary, in 1990. President Bush received congressional approval for possible military action on January 16, 1991. He ordered the multinational invasion of Kuwait called Operation Desert Storm to begin the next day, January 17.

★

THE ALLIED COALITION had approximately 1,700 aircraft poised to attack Iraqi forces. Apache helicopter gunships and Stealth fighters went into service. Though the Stealths were designed to be invisible to radar, the U.S. Air Force took no chances and jammed enemy radar. Unfortunately, the jamming alerted the Iraqis that something was happening, and Hussein ordered blind firing of missiles without even knowing the target.

★

IN LATE JANUARY, Hussein ordered his troops to open a Kuwaiti pipeline, pouring petroleum into the Persian Gulf. The oil not only damaged the environment, but also threatened the desalination plants that provided drinking water to Saudi Arabia. U.S. bombing raids managed to curtail the pipeline damage, but the oil had already done great harm to the water, beaches, and sea life.

ON FEBRUARY 24, the ground war began as U.S. Marines penetrated Iraqi lines and pushed to liberate Kuwait City. As fleeing Iraqi soldiers moved back toward their border, U.S. forces dropped a string of bombs on the convoy, stalling it. On the third day of the ground war, the U.S. Seventh Corps caught up with the Iraqi Republican Guard Division. Tank fighting was heavy, but the U.S. equipment was far superior to the Soviet-made tanks that Iraq used. Other defeats soon followed, and the Iraqi troops retreated.

IN THE MONTHS after the Gulf War, President Bush enjoyed a 90 percent approval rating among Americans. As the months wore on to the 1992 election, however, it became evident that although Bush handled foreign relations well, his comprehension didn't extend to his electorate, who resented his inaction on domestic matters.

COMPARED TO OTHER wars' casualty numbers, the Allied casualty count from the Gulf War was relatively low: a total of 149 Allied soldiers died in the line of duty, and a little more than 500 were wounded. Iraqi casualties were much higher, with estimates ranging from 25,000 to 100,000.

SEVERAL EVENTS MADE headlines at this time in mainstream America. Headline News itself was newsworthy as an offshoot of the Cable News Network (CNN), created by Ted Turner, an Atlanta businessman, in 1980. When others fled, CNN reporter Peter Arnett and others remained in Iraq and brought the air raids and Scud missile launches into people's homes as they occurred tens of thousands of miles away. Headline News ran half-hour capsulated versions of important news each day.

MOUNT SAINT HELENS, a volcano in the Cascade Range of Washington state that had been dormant for more than 120 years, erupted on May 18, 1980, with rock and debris spewing twelve miles, and volcanic ash much farther. Rumbles had been heard early in the year, but the sudden eruption measured 4.1 on the Richter scale. It blew off the top of the 9,675-foot peak, causing flooding, mudslides, and billions of dollars in property damage.

MILLIONS WATCHED THE ROYAL WEDDING of Britain's Prince Charles and Lady Diana Spencer. Americans quickly took a liking to the young princess, following the births of her children, her rise as a fashion icon and humanitarian, her divorce, and her tragic death in an automobile accident in 1997.

AIDS (ACQUIRED IMMUNODEFICIENCY SYNDROME) and HIV (human immunodeficiency virus, which causes AIDS) came to everyone's attention in the mid-1980s as the killer virus was identified almost simultaneously at the Pasteur Institute in Paris and at the National Cancer Institute in Bethesda, Maryland. Actor Rock Hudson died of the disease in 1985; this loss and others galvanized those fighting for adequate research. More than 25 million people have died as a result of AIDS since 1981.

---- ★ ----

THE SPACE SHUTTLE *Challenger*, with a crew of seven astronauts featuring America's first civilian and teacher sent into space, exploded in a burst of flames only seventy-three seconds into its flight on January 28, 1986. Mission commander Francis R. Scobee; pilot Michael J. Smith; mission specialists Ronald E. McNair, Ellison S. Onizuka, and Judith A. Resnik; and payload specialists Gregory B. Jarvis and Sharon Christa McAuliffe, a high school teacher from New Hampshire, all perished in the accident.

---- ★ ----

THE *CHALLENGER* TRAGEDY halted the launch program until designers modified the shuttle and implemented tighter safety measures. Shuttle missions resumed on September 28, 1988, with the flight of the space shuttle *Discovery*.

---- ★ ----

ON THE NIGHT of March 24, 1989, the *Exxon Valdez*, an American oil tanker, went aground on a reef in Prince William Sound, Alaska. The 987-foot tanker began leaking oil in a spill that continued for two days, making it the worst oil disaster of its kind in U.S. history. Approximately 1,100 miles of Alaskan shoreline was contaminated, killing birds, sea mammals, and fish. The captain of the tanker not only lost his job amid allegations of a substance-abuse problem, but faced criminal charges in the matter as well.

---- ★ ----

A SAN FRANCISCO EARTHQUAKE measuring 6.9 on the Richter scale struck the city as baseball fans were finding their seats for the third game of the World Series, October 17, 1989. The tremor erupted along the San Andreas Fault. Although it lasted a mere fifteen seconds, it resulted in collapsed highways, dozens of deaths, and billions of dollars in property damage.

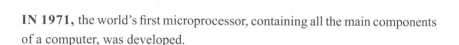

IN 1971, the world's first microprocessor, containing all the main components of a computer, was developed.

***

THROUGHOUT THE '80s, the chips became smaller and smaller, so computers became more and more affordable and convenient for business and home use. Cheap mass production brought forth handheld electronic gadgets that transformed everyday life. Calculators, once the size of a box on a desk, shrank to the size of a credit card.

***

AT THE FOREFRONT of this technological revolution were two young entrepreneurial spirits—Steve Jobs and Steve Wozniak—both Californians with no special programming or electronics knowledge. Working together in a garage, in 1977 they developed the first user-friendly computer, designed for mass marketing rather than big business, called the Apple II. It was followed by the Macintosh in 1984. Jobs and Wozniak named their operation the Apple Computer Company.

***

A HARVARD DROPOUT, Bill Gates, with his company Microsoft, was hired by IBM (International Business Machines) to develop an operating system for the corporation's computers, which was called MS-DOS. IBM, which had built personal computers, or "PCs," in 1981 around the latest Intel microprocessor, failed to claim exclusive rights for MS-DOS, and soon, Microsoft developed its own GUI system with Windows 3.0 software.

***

GATES HELPED OTHER companies use reverse engineering to circumvent patent law, creating almost identical computers (or clones) of the IBM hardware. Today, IBM compatibles are widely seen in stores, homes, and business, making Bill Gates one of the richest men in the world.

———— ★ ————

IN 1963, BILL CLINTON was elected as an Arkansas delegate to Boys Nation, a government study program for youth in Washington, DC, where he shook President John F. Kennedy's hand at a White House Rose Garden ceremony. This famous photo was displayed during the Democratic National Convention in 1992 as the party depicted Clinton as the boy from Hope, Arkansas.

———— ★ ————

ROSS PEROT DROPPED out of the presidential race in July 1992, citing personal and family reasons, only to re-enter in October. That November, he received 19 percent of the national vote, the highest percentage any independent candidate had won. Had those who voted for the third-party candidate favored the president, Bush would have won in a landslide. But the new kid on the block won this election—Bill Clinton garnered 43 percent of the popular vote and a majority of the Electoral College.

———— ★ ————

TO WIN ELECTION, Bill Clinton capitalized on a certain charisma he had, being the first of the baby boom generation to be elected to the presidency. He appointed more women and minorities to high government office and cabinet posts than any previous president. Among his appointments were Attorney General Janet Reno, Secretary of Agriculture Mike Espy, Secretary of Commerce Ron Brown, Secretary of Health and Human Services Donna Shalala, and two new Supreme Court justices, Stephen G. Breyer and Ruth

Bader Ginsburg. Madeleine Albright became the first female secretary of state during Clinton's second term in office.

— ★ —

A RHODES SCHOLAR is someone who attends Oxford University on a scholarship funded over a century ago by diamond tycoon Cecil Rhodes. It is a very prestigious program. President Clinton is the only American president to have ever received a Rhodes scholarship.

— ★ —

CONNECTICUT IS HOME to Yale University, one of the most prestigious colleges in the world. Up to this point, the last three presidents—George H. W. Bush, George W. Bush, and Bill Clinton—all attended Yale.

— ★ —

FROM THE START, it seemed that Clinton had well-organized enemies. Questions were posed regarding failed real estate dealings the Clintons had been involved with in Arkansas, which became known as the Whitewater scandal. A second scandal faced the president when a former Arkansas state employee, Paula Jones, filed suit alleging sexual harassment during Clinton's tenure as governor.

— ★ —

PRESIDENT CLINTON'S WIFE, Hillary, is the first first lady ever to hold elective office. She's also the first first lady to serve in Congress and the first female senator from New York.

— ★ —

CLINTON REMAINED POPULAR among women for his advocacy of their concerns. He overturned restrictions on abortions and signed into law a family leave bill requiring companies with more than fifty workers to allow parents up to twelve weeks of unpaid leave a year to cope with family issues. Clinton tackled discrimination against homosexuals in the armed forces with a policy that would become known as "Don't Ask, Don't Tell."

———————— ★ ————————

THE "DON'T ASK, DON'T TELL" policy was the compromise that President Bill Clinton and the Joint Chiefs of Staff reached concerning homosexuals in the armed forces. Although the ban remained in effect, the military could not ask if a person was homosexual.

———————— ★ ————————

IN 1987, GINGRICH initiated ethics charges against Speaker of the House Jim Wright, eventually leading to Wright's resignation. Gingrich's passionate pursuit of shrinking the federal government (his "Contract with America") was widely publicized, enabling his fellow Republicans to gain control of both the House and the Senate in the 1994 elections. Gingrich was later reprimanded in 1997 by House members for ethics violations, giving false information, and using tax-exempt donations for political activities.

———————— ★ ————————

CLINTON AND CONGRESS were successful at passing the presidential line-item veto, which allowed the president to veto individual items on appropriations bills. But this was challenged in court as being unconstitutional. Many measures were halted by the president's veto or threatened veto of Republican initiatives.

———————— ★ ————————

CLINTON AND CONGRESS were unable to reach an agreement on the federal budget for 1996. Debate brewed over how to reform welfare, Medicare, Medicaid, and other programs. The result was two partial shutdowns of the federal government. Finally, Clinton and Congress agreed on budget concessions. Republicans got the spending cuts they wanted, but Clinton managed to maintain educational and environmental programs that the administration deemed vital. Clinton did sign an increase in the minimum wage, as well as making it easier for workers to transfer from one employer's health insurance to another without losing coverage (even with a pre-existing condition). Clinton also overhauled the welfare program, which had been a 1992 campaign promise.

---------- ★ ----------

AS A MEMBER of Congress, Al Gore earned a reputation for his stand on environmental issues, pioneering efforts to clean up hazardous waste dumps and prevent depletion of the earth's ozone layer. He wrote *Earth in the Balance: Ecology and the Human Spirit*, published in 1992, and served as vice president under Bill Clinton from 1993–2001.

---------- ★ ----------

CLINTON ALSO LOBBIED hard for sweeping trade legislation lowering the barriers to trade with other nations. In doing so, he faced the opposition of many supporters, including trade unions, as they feared American jobs would be lost to a cheaper labor market. But Clinton maintained, despite vigorous debate with H. Ross Perot during the 1992 campaign, that the North American Free Trade Agreement (NAFTA) was necessary. Clinton persuaded members of his own party to join in the largely Republican-backed legislative vote. The treaty was passed in the House of Representatives in November 1993. In foreign affairs, Clinton helped secure peace in Haiti by reinstating ousted president Jean-Bertrand Aristide.

———————— ★ ————————

A CAR BOMB left in an underground parking garage exploded in the heart of New York City's financial district in February of 1993. The World Trade Center bombing killed six people, injured more than 1,000 others, and caused around $600 million worth of damage. In 1994, four members of a militant Islamic group were convicted in connection with the previous year's car bombing.

———————— ★ ————————

TEN MUSLIM MILITANTS were convicted of conspiring in 1994 to bomb the United Nations headquarters, two tunnels, and other prominent New York landmarks. Their convictions were handed down in 1995.

———————— ★ ————————

IN 1993, MEMBERS OF A HEAVILY ARMED RELIGIOUS SECT calling themselves the Branch Davidians held a fifty-one-day standoff with law-enforcement officials near Waco, Texas. When negotiations failed, federal agents stormed the complex, resulting in the death of eighty Branch Davidians and four agents. Attorney General Janet Reno accepted responsibility for giving the go-ahead.

———————— ★ ————————

ON APRIL 19, 1995, terrorism struck in America's heartland. A blast caused by a huge car bomb blew open one whole side of the Alfred P. Murrah Federal Building in Oklahoma City, killing more than 168 people, at least fifteen of whom were children in day care. It was the worst act of terrorism on U.S. soil at that time.

———————— ★ ————————

THE FBI ARRESTED their key suspect for the Oklahoma City bombing, twenty-seven-year-old Timothy McVeigh, who harbored a far-right political agenda and alliances to paramilitary groups. Terry Nichols was also charged in the crime. Believers in this extremist group encouraged others to stockpile weapons, because they feared the government was plotting to take away their rights.

———————— ★ ————————

DURING THE 1996 SUMMER OLYMPICS held in Atlanta, Georgia, a pipe bomb exploded in an outdoor park. Eric Rudolph of North Carolina was finally caught in 2003 and convicted in 2005 for the crime. Also in 1996, the FBI finally caught up to a mail bomber, Ted Kaczynski, in the back woods of Montana. Authorities had been chasing after the "Unabomber" for twenty years. Both men are serving multiple life sentences.

———————— ★ ————————

THOUGH INAUGURATION DAY is steeped in tradition, there have been many "firsts" throughout the years. Herbert Hoover was the first to have his inauguration captured on "talking newsreel," while Harry Truman's was the first televised inauguration. Bill Clinton was the first president to have his ceremony broadcast live over the Internet.

———————— ★ ————————

CLINTON'S SECOND TERM was markedly marred by scandal. In the spring of 1999, the Paula Jones case finally reached an $850,000 settlement, with Ms. Jones's attorneys collecting much of the money. In her lawsuit, Paula Jones claimed that President Clinton, then Governor Clinton, made sexual advances toward her in a Little Rock, Arkansas, hotel room in 1991. Clinton steadfastly denied the accusation. Although the case had been dismissed, it was in the appeals process at the time Clinton and Ms. Jones reached a settlement.

DURING A DEPOSITION in the Paula Jones case, however, Clinton had testified that he had not had a relationship with a former White House intern named Monica Lewinsky. Ms. Lewinsky had begun work at the White House in June 1995, later becoming a salaried employee in the White House Office of Legislative Affairs. Unfortunately for the president, she spoke rather freely with a friend named Linda Tripp, a government civil servant, who quietly taped their assorted (and sometimes sordid) telephone conversations. Lewinsky told Tripp of her trysts with the president in the Oval Office, sometimes in gossipy, graphic detail.

★

THE CLINTON–LEWINSKY EXTRAMARITAL AFFAIR was exposed by Kenneth Starr, the independent counsel originally hired to investigate the Whitewater matter. But that investigation moved in convoluted directions. Some say that his motives were purely political and that he had clients directly opposed to the Clinton administration. Indeed the White House called his attacks and probing "fishing expeditions."

★

IN THE 1990s, the information superhighway had average Americans surfing the Net. The Internet was developed in 1969 by the defense department, military, and universities to link up computers in remote areas. But in the 1990s, almost every government agency and private enterprise started a site on the World Wide Web. "Dot-com" stocks soared in the midst of the frenzy.

★

BECAUSE CLINTON HAD given false statements under oath, impeachment proceedings began in the House of Representatives (with a vote that was largely split among party lines), followed by a trial in the Senate in 1999. Clinton became known in the history books as the second president ever to be impeached. He was acquitted in his Senate trial, and so was not removed from office.

★

DURING THE 1990s, America witnessed the age of celebrity. It seemed that if you could make a name for yourself—whether it be as an Olympic champion or prime athlete, a television talk show host or box-office favorite, or even a jilted lover or victim of a horrendous crime—you could cash in on that celebrity status. Among the favorites were teen heartthrobs such as Leonardo DiCaprio, star of the movie *Titanic*, which became the biggest box-office hit in history at the time and grossed more than $1 billion, and basketball player Michael Jordan.

★

IN APRIL 1999, two young men tossed homemade bombs and fired bullets throughout Columbine High School in Littleton, Colorado. The rampage left twelve young people and one teacher dead, with many others injured, both physically and psychologically. It became overwhelmingly clear that many troubled youth had easy access to weapons, found potentially lethal information such as how to make pipe bombs on the Internet, and enjoyed violent themes in the music they listened to and the films they viewed.

★

AS THE YEAR 2000 APPROACHED, everyone wondered if the turn of the century would bring with it massive infrastructure problems. Computers and computer software, the mainstay of most business, government, military, and nonprofit operations, had to be retooled for the new century. People feared that when the clock struck midnight, computer systems would fail to recognize the "00" and create havoc worldwide. Banking establishments, utilities, governments, and other entities spent millions of dollars during the later part of the 1990s preparing for "Y2K."

IN HONOR OF THE NEW MILLENNIUM, OpSail 2000 attracted curious onlookers and sea-loving fans of the tall ships. The official ports for the ships included San Juan, Puerto Rico; Miami, Florida; Hampton Roads, Virginia; Baltimore, Maryland; Philadelphia, Pennsylvania; New York, New York; New London, Connecticut; and Portland, Maine. The official national celebration occurred in New York Harbor during the Fourth of July weekend.

OPSAIL 2000 WAS dubbed the "greatest event in maritime history"; the last time the tall ships had assembled together was for the Bicentennial celebration in 1976.

OPERATION SAIL WAS founded by President John F. Kennedy, who said in 1962, "The sight of so many ships gathered from distant corners of the world for Operation Sail should remind us that strong, disciplined, and adventuresome men still can find their way safely across uncertain and stormy seas." Of course, Kennedy, being a naval hero, was a little partial to those who plied the seas!

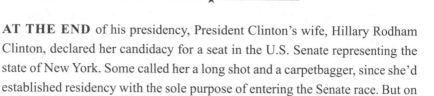

AT THE END of his presidency, President Clinton's wife, Hillary Rodham Clinton, declared her candidacy for a seat in the U.S. Senate representing the state of New York. Some called her a long shot and a carpetbagger, since she'd established residency with the sole purpose of entering the Senate race. But on November 7, 2000, she prevailed.

DEMOCRATIC VICE PRESIDENT Al Gore ran against the Republican governor George W. Bush of Texas, son of the former president. Even before the election, with polls so close that analysts couldn't make accurate predictions, some were remembering earlier presidential elections such as the 1888 race between Grover Cleveland, who won the popular vote, and Benjamin Harrison, who prevailed in the Electoral College.

IN ORDER TO win the presidency, a candidate must garner at least 270 electoral votes.

TELEVISION NETWORKS WERE far too quick to call the president race. Early in the evening, it appeared Vice President Gore was leading in electoral votes, but this margin later slipped. In the wee hours of the morning, the television networks called George W. Bush the winner, and Gore even telephoned him to concede the race. A short time later, Gore learned that the race was too close to call in the state of Florida. He telephoned Bush again and revoked his concession.

ALL EYES FELL on Florida's twenty-five electoral votes, for they would decide the next president. Never before in American history was an election undecided for days and weeks after voters had gone to the polls. It appeared that Gore had more popular votes and Bush more electoral ones (he had 271 of the 270 required if he carried Florida). Everything from absentee ballots and ballot design in certain Florida counties to the way in which the ballots were punched and counted came under the microscope, with each side engaging attorneys to urge or fight a potential recount.

IN THE 2000 presidential election, there were 543,895 more popular votes for Senator Al Gore than for Governor George Bush, but George Bush won the election by five electoral votes.

ON DECEMBER 12, 2000—the deadline for Florida to certify its twenty-five electors—the U.S. Supreme Court, in a 5-to-4 ruling, declared that the counting of the disputed votes had to be completed by midnight. This essentially handed the election to George W. Bush. Vice President Al Gore, in an address to the American people, graciously conceded the race while holding firm to his belief that every vote should have been counted. He also pledged his support to the incoming administration.

PRESIDENT BUSH LOVES baseball so much that while his father was president he bought a controlling interest in the Texas Rangers and ran it as majority owner from 1989 to 1993. He is the only president to have owned a sports team.

THE TOP ITEM on Bush's domestic agenda, and a major campaign promise, a $1.6 trillion tax cut, was the subject of bitter debate in Congress. While Bush and his supporters claimed that the tax cuts would promote new investment and economic growth, the Democrats argued that the bill heavily favored the rich and would waste away the unprecedented budget surplus. The Senate eventually trimmed the tax cut to $1.35 trillion over eleven years, and Bush signed it into law on June 7.

ALMOST 60 PERCENT of George Bush's tax cuts were limited to the wealthiest 10 percent of Americans, with the richest 1 percent of Americans receiving nearly 45 percent of the tax cuts. By November of 2006, the national debt was 8,599,573,549,780 and growing by $2.55 billion each day.

IN THE FINAL two years of the Clinton administration, there were budget surpluses of $122.7 billion (1999) and $230 billion (2000). As a result of the surpluses, the $5.7 trillion national debt had been reduced by $360 billion in the previous three years.

THE BUSH TAX LAW was a plan to send checks to 95 million people. Those advanced payments were referred to as "tax rebates." The rebates ranged from $300 to $600 depending on whether someone was single, married, or the head of a household. The total cost of the rebates was approximately $38 billion dollars. By the time Americans began receiving their tax rebate checks in August 2001, the country's budget surplus was beginning to disappear. The Congressional Budget Office attributed the change to a slowing economy and the Bush tax cut. By the fall, many believed that the country was heading toward a full-blown recession.

EARLY IN HIS ADMINISTRATION, Bush and his advisers considered the oil supply essential to the health and profitability of leading U.S. industries. This concern prompted Bush to establish the National Energy Policy Development Group (NEPDG) and Vice President Richard Cheney was selected to lead the task force. Early on it appeared that the choice facing the policy planners was becoming ever more dependent on imported supplies or choosing the alternate route of reliance on renewable sources of energy and gradually reducing petroleum use.

——————— ★ ———————

THE NATIONAL ENERGY POLICY DEVELOPMENT GROUP completed its report during the early months of 2001. At first glance, the Cheney report, as it is often called, appeared to reject the path of increased reliance on imported oil in favor of renewable energy. However, for all its rhetoric about conservation, the report did not propose a reduction in oil consumption. Instead, it proposed to boost production at home through the exploitation of untapped reserves in protected wilderness areas, including the Arctic National Wildlife Refuge (ANWR), an immense, untouched wilderness area in northeastern Alaska.

——————— ★ ———————

THE GENERAL ACCOUNTING OFFICE, the investigative arm of Congress, requested information in spring of 2001 about which industry executives and lobbyists the Task Force was meeting with in developing the Bush administration's energy plan. When Cheney refused disclosure, Congress was pressed to sue for the right to examine Task Force records, but lost. Later, amid political pressure building over improprieties regarding Enron's colossal collapse, Cheney's office released limited information revealing six Task Force meetings with Enron executives.

——————— ★ ———————

AT 8:45 A.M. ON SEPTEMBER 11, 2001, a hijacked passenger jet, American Airlines Flight 11 out of Boston's Logan Airport, crashed into the north tower of the World Trade Center, tearing a gaping hole in the building and setting it afire. As people watched the burning tower in horror, a second hijacked airliner, United Airlines Flight 175 from Boston, crashed into the south tower of the World Trade Center at 9:03 A.M. and exploded. Both buildings were now in flames. At approximately 9:43 A.M., American Airlines Flight 77 out of Washington exploded when it hit the Pentagon, killing all sixty-four people aboard. At 10:05 A.M. the south tower fell, sending a huge cloud of dust and debris through the streets of lower Manhattan. At 10:10 A.M. United Airlines Flight 93 out of Newark and bound for San Francisco, also hijacked, crashed in Somerset County, Pennsylvania, southeast of Pittsburgh, killing the thirty-eight passengers, crew, and hijackers. At 10:28 A.M. the north tower of the World Trade Center collapsed.

—————————— ★ ——————————

SEPTEMBER 11, 2001, marked the largest single-day loss of life in United States history.

—————————— ★ ——————————

SHORTLY AFTER THE ATTACKS OF SEPTEMBER 11, the terrorist group Al-Qaeda, under the leadership of Osama bin Laden, was suspected of being responsible. Al-Qaeda has its origins in the uprising against the 1979 Soviet occupation of Afghanistan. After the Soviets left Afghanistan, bin Laden returned to his native Saudi Arabia and then later set up bases in Sudan in northeast Africa. In 1994 Sudan expelled bin Laden, who moved his base of operations to Afghanistan. Bin Laden was welcomed by the Taliban ("Students of Islamic Knowledge Movement") who came to power during Afghanistan's long civil war and ruled Afghanistan from 1996 until 2001. The United States drove them from power in November of 2001.

BIN LADEN EXPLAINED the origin of the term "Al-Qaeda" in a videotaped interview with an Al Jazeera (Arabic television channel) journalist in October 2001: "The name 'al-Qaeda' was established a long time ago by mere chance. The late Abu Ebeida El-Banashiri established the training camps for our mujahedeed against Russia's terrorism. We used to call the training camp al-Qaeda [meaning "the base" in English]. And the name stayed."

★

IN FEBRUARY 1993, Al-Qaeda had bombed the World Trade Center in New York City. The 1,500-pound nitrate-fuel oil device killed six and injured 1,042 people. It was intended to devastate the foundation of the north tower, causing it to collapse onto the south tower; six people were killed. Those involved in the bombing received financing from Al-Qaeda member Khalid Shaikh Mohammed. Investigation of the WTC bombing revealed that it was only a small part of a massive attack plan that included hijacking a plane and crashing it into CIA headquarters.

★

IN OCTOBER 1993, Al-Qaeda killed U.S. soldiers in Somalia. Bin Laden confirmed that "Arabs affiliated with his group were involved in killing American troops in Somalia in 1993," a claim he had earlier made to an Arabic newspaper. The Battle of Mogadishu was the basis of the film *Black Hawk Down*.

★

IN AUGUST 1998, Al-Qaeda bombed two U.S. embassies in Africa. On August 7, 1998, terrorists bombed the U.S. embassies in Nairobi, Kenya, and Dar es Salaam, Tanzania, leaving 258 people dead and more than 5,000 injured.

President Clinton demonstrated an aggressive response as the United States launched cruise missiles on August 20, 1998, striking a terrorism training complex in Afghanistan and destroying a pharmaceutical manufacturing facility in Khartoum, Sudan, that reportedly produced poison gases for military use, both believed to be financed by Osama bin Laden. Officials later said that there was no proof that the plant had been manufacturing or storing nerve gas, as initially suspected by the Americans, or had been linked to Osama bin Laden, who was a resident of Khartoum in the 1980s.

ON OCTOBER 12, 2000, seventeen Americans died and thirty-seven were wounded when suicide bombers attacked the U.S. Navy destroyer *Cole*, which was refueling in Aden, Yemen. It appeared that the small boat carrying the suicide bombers was carrying some form of high explosive material powerful enough to rip a large hole, forty by sixty feet, flooding the main engine spaces of the ship.

ON THE MORNING of June 14, 2002, a truck with a fertilizer bomb driven by a suicide bomber was detonated outside the U.S. Consulate in Karachi, Pakistan. Twelve people were killed and fifty-one injured, all Pakistanis.

IN JUNE 2004, terrorists kidnapped and executed (by beheading) Paul Johnson Jr., an American helicopter engineer, in Riyadh, Saudi Arabia.

IN DECEMBER 2004, militants, believed to be linked to Al-Qaeda, drove up to the U.S. consulate in Jiddah, Saudi Arabia, stormed the gates, and killed five consulate employees, none of whom were American. Saudi security forces subdued the attackers, killing four.

IN JULY 2005, four young suicide bombers with possible ties to Al-Qaeda struck in central London on July 7, 2005, killing fifty-two people and injuring more than 770.

ON OCTOBER 7, 2001, after the Taliban failed to respond to their demands, the United States, Great Britain, and coalition forces launched a bombing campaign on the Taliban government and Al-Qaeda terrorist camps in Afghanistan. Although the immediate goal was to destroy Al-Qaeda and capture bin Laden, the president stated that the "battle was broader." Perhaps the intentions of the administration were already on Iraq. Within two months the Taliban government had fallen. Although Osama bin Laden was not caught, the Al-Qaeda forces in Afghanistan were seriously weakened.

FORTY-FIVE DAYS AFTER the September 11 attacks, Congress, with little if any debate, passed the 342-page USA PATRIOT Act (Uniting and Strengthening America by Providing Appropriate Tools Required to Intercept and Obstruct Terrorism Act). The vote in the House of Representatives was 357 to 66 and in the Senate 98 to 1, with Senator Russ Feingold of Wisconsin being the only senator to vote against the act.

SINCE ITS PASSAGE, nearly 200 cities/towns and three states have passed resolutions stating that the Patriot Act is not enforceable within their jurisdictions, claiming that among other concerns, the First, Fourth, Fifth, Sixth, Eighth, and Fourteenth Amendments are being threatened. The USA Patriot Act has raised the tension that exists when a country is at war and national security is pitted against civil liberties. The balance that must be maintained is the protection and security of society without sacrificing the very system that is being kept secure. Following successful constitutional challenges to some sections of the act, the Patriot Act was renewed in March 2006.

SECTION 213 OF THE USA PATRIOT ACT contains the first authorization for the issuance of "sneak and peek" search warrants in American history. These warrants allow search and seizure without notifying the individual being searched at the time of the search. This section is not restricted to terrorists or terrorism offenses; it may be used in connection with any federal crime, including misdemeanors.

ON NOVEMBER 25, 2002, President Bush signed into law legislation creating a new cabinet-level Department of Homeland Security and appointed Tom Ridge, ex-governor of Pennsylvania, as secretary of homeland security.

ON DECEMBER 22, 2001, Hamid Karzai, who attended college in India, speaks fluent English, and enjoys strong support from the West, was sworn in as interim chairman of the government. Karzai initially supported the Taliban and is respected by many former Taliban leaders. Karzai was a candidate in the October 9, 2004, Afghanistan presidential elections. He won twenty-one of the thirty-four provinces, becoming the first democratically elected leader of Afghanistan. The Taliban demonstrated resurgence in 2006 and remains a very credible force within Afghanistan.

THE MILITARY INVASION OF IRAQ set to begin on March 19, 2003, at 9:34 P.M., Eastern Standard Time, was known as Operation Iraqi Freedom. These military operations would be against the state of Iraq to rid the country of its weapons of mass destruction and remove Saddam Hussein and his government from power. On February 26, 2003, President George W. Bush denounced North Korea, Iran, and Iraq as dangers to the rest of the world and warned that the United States would wage war against countries developing weapons of mass destruction. There were parts of his address that were later found to be untrue; for example, the president stated, "Our discoveries in Afghanistan confirmed our worst fears and showed us the true scope of the task ahead. We have found diagrams of American nuclear power plants."

———————— ★ ————————

THE STATE OF THE UNION ADDRESS by Presidents of the United States is mandated by the United States Constitution. George Washington's first State of the Union was probably the shortest, only 833 words, which most likely took four to seven minutes to deliver. The longest State of the Union was by Harry Truman in 1946; his speech was over 25,000 words!

———————— ★ ————————

ON MAY 14, 2002, the United Nations Security Council replaced sanctions on Iraq with "smart sanctions." "Smart sanctions" were meant to allow food, medical supplies, and goods into the country while restricting any trade that could be used for military purposes. These sanctions were designed to force Iraq to comply with United Nations resolutions about weapons of mass destruction. At the time, it was estimated by the United Nations that the sanctions had resulted in the deaths of over 1 million Iraqi civilians.

———————— ★ ————————

ON SEPTEMBER 12, 2002, President Bush addressed the United Nations and called for "regime change" in Iraq. Interestingly enough, the goal of regime change in Iraq was codified during the Clinton years with the passage of the Iraq Liberation Act in 1998, which stated that "it should be the policy of the United States to support efforts to remove the regime headed by Saddam Hussein from power in Iraq and to promote the emergence of a democratic government to replace that regime."

———————— ★ ————————

ON OCTOBER 11, 2002, Congress passed the Joint Resolution to Authorize the Use of United States Armed Forces Against Iraq. On November 8, 2002, the United Nations Security Council passed a unanimous resolution calling for tough new arms inspections and demanding that Iraq disarm or face serious consequences. This was followed by the return of United Nations weapons inspectors to Iraq for the first time in nearly four years. On December 7, 2002, Iraq submitted a statement on its chemical, biological, and nuclear capabilities, claiming it possessed no banned weapons.

———————— ★ ————————

ON NOVEMBER 8, 2002, the United Nations Security Council passed a unanimous resolution calling on Iraq to disarm or face "serious consequences." United Nations arms inspectors were sent back to Iraq. On December 7, 2002, Iran submitted to the United Nations a lengthy declaration stating that it had no weapons that had been banned. In mid-January, United Nations inspectors discovered undeclared empty chemical warheads. During January, President Bush received a letter signed by 130 members of the House of Representatives, urging him to "let the inspectors work." By this time, nearly 200,000 United States troops were in the Middle East region.

———————— ★ ————————

ON JANUARY 28, 2003, Bush delivered his State of the Union address and stated that Iraq was attempting to buy uranium from Africa, even though he already had the intelligence that Iraq had not done so. By February, United Nations weapons inspector Hans Blix indicated that there was some progress with Iraq's compliance. Later that month, the United States, Britain, and Spain submitted a proposed resolution to the United Nations Security Council that authorization for war was necessary. Germany, Russia, and France opposed the resolution. By March 14, 2003, the council had only four out of the necessary nine votes to support military action.

★

ON FEBRUARY 15, 2003, "The World Says No to War" protest took place, with massive peace demonstrations around the world. It was the largest coordinated day of protest in world history, with more than 600 cities participating. In Rome alone nearly 3 million people protested, which is noted in *Guinness World Records* as the largest antiwar rally in history.

★

ON MARCH 19, 2003, President Bush declared war on Iraq without a United Nations Mandate, as he said he would in his State of the Union address on January 28, and Operation Iraqi Freedom was commenced. Secretary of Defense Donald Rumsfeld addressed concerns about the war, saying, "What will follow will not be a repeat of any other conflict. It will be of a force and a scope and a scale that has been beyond what we have seen before." Unfortunately, Secretary Rumsfeld's prediction of a swift and efficient victory in Iraq had not come to be, as the Iraq War lasted longer than our involvement in World War II. By December 2011, the United States government withdrew its troops from Iraq.

★

IN DECEMBER, 2001, Enron, the largest energy corporation in the United States, filed for bankruptcy. Prior to this, Enron had been investigated for illegally driving up power prices during California's energy crisis. Enron had been under federal investigation for "cooking the books"—that is, falsifying higher earnings and hiding the company's debt. Perhaps the greatest tragedy was the loss of its employees' retirement funds. In 2002 WorldCom, a major telecommunications corporation, went bankrupt after admitting to illegally altering its earnings and debt reports. Following Enron and WorldCom came charges against Qwest, Global Crossing, Tyco, and Adelphia, as corporate America came under intense scrutiny for illegal activities, incredible greed, and criminal disregard for its employees.

------------ ★ ------------

ON DECEMBER 13, 2001, President Bush gave notice that the United States would be withdrawing from the Anti–Ballistic Missile Treaty, marking the first time in recent history that the United States has withdrawn from a major international arms treaty. The United States withdrew on June 13, 2002.

------------ ★ ------------

THE INTERNATIONAL CRIMINAL COURT was established on July 17, 1998. Today, 104 countries have submitted to the jurisdiction of the ICC. The court is based in The Hague, Netherlands, and hears cases involving international law, including allegations of genocide, crimes against humanity, and war crimes. To date, the United States has not ratified the ICC, arguing that prosecutions may be brought against U.S. nationals for political reasons.

------------ ★ ------------

THE KYOTO PROTOCOL (named for the city of Kyoto, Japan), which, for the first time, would require certain nations to cut the emissions of gases that contribute to global warming, was never ratified by the Senate when President

Clinton was in office. After assuming office in January 2001, President George W. Bush announced that the United States would withdraw from the Kyoto Treaty. As late as 2005, the Bush administration was still stating that there were many "inconsistencies" in reports that global warming was taking place.

IN DECEMBER 2002, nine states—New York, Connecticut, Maine, Maryland, Massachusetts, New Hampshire, New Jersey, Rhode Island, and Vermont—brought a lawsuit against the Environmental Protection Agency that challenged new regulations of the Bush administration that would remove some of the protections of the 1970 Clean Air Act.

THE HOLDING OF THE SUPREME COURT in Atkins v. Virginia, decided on June 25, 2002, found that the execution of mentally retarded individuals was a "cruel and unusual punishment" prohibited by the Eighth Amendment.

ON FEBRUARY 1, 2003, the space shuttle *Columbia* exploded in the skies over Texas as it was re-entering the earth's atmosphere. All seven crewmembers were killed in the disaster.

ON JANUARY 10, 2003, North Korea announced that they were withdrawing from the Nuclear Nonproliferation Treaty, following accusations made by the United States that the country was engaged in nuclear weapons programs. North Korea had ratified the treaty in 1985 and was the first country ever to withdraw from the treaty.

ON MAY 1, 2003, President Bush announced from the deck of the aircraft carrier USS *Abraham Lincoln* that major combat operations in Iraq were over. Behind him was a banner proclaiming "Mission Accomplished," and the president hailed a "job well done."

There has been much controversy over this event and the president's claim of victory in Iraq. Although the White House first said that it was the navy who put up the banner, later reports from the White House stated that they had it made for the navy to put up on the ship. In retrospect, all agree the announcement was unfortunately premature.

SADDAM HUSSEIN, at age sixty-six, was captured by American troops on December 13, 2003. He was found hiding in a dirt hole at a farmhouse about ten miles south of his hometown, Tikrit. Saddam Hussein had not been seen since Baghdad fell to coalition forces in April 2003.

THE 2004 PRESIDENTIAL ELECTION was the closest re-election campaign in American history.

WHILE THE RESULTS of the election were contested (many, including members of Congress, felt that the count in Ohio was wrong and that many voters were intentionally kept from the polls), in the end it was a very tight victory for the incumbent administration of George Bush and Dick Cheney. Kerry and Edwards had lost by two percent.

ON MARCH 29, 2004, the North Atlantic Treaty Organization (NATO) admitted seven former communist eastern European countries: Bulgaria, Estonia, Latvia, Lithuania, Romania, Slovakia, and Slovenia. On April 1, 2009, Albania and Croatia were admitted. With the admission of these nine countries, NATO now has twenty-eight members.

———————— ★ ————————

ON APRIL 30, 2004, it was revealed that United States military personnel were torturing, abusing, and sexually humiliating Iraqi prisoners at the Abu Ghraib prison, a facility about twenty miles west of Baghdad. Photographs from Abu Ghraib caused outrage and anti-American sentiments around the world. The administration condemned the acts and said that they were the responsibility of a small group of low-level military personnel.

———————— ★ ————————

ON THE DAY after Christmas, 2004, an earthquake (9.3 on the Richter scale) under the Indian Ocean produced a number of tsunami waves that devastated coastal communities in Southeast Asia, including Indonesia, Thailand, India, and Sri Lanka. The death toll was estimated at over 220,000 people. An outpouring of worldwide aid totaling $7 billion to the area followed.

———————— ★ ————————

ON FEBRUARY 4, 2004, Massachusetts became the first state in the country to permit same-sex marriages on an equal basis with heterosexual marriages. The court's ruling gave the legislature six months to rewrite the law and rid the statute of language that banned same-sex marriage.

———————— ★ ————————

GEORGE W. BUSH was officially sworn in for his second term as president on January 20, 2005. After taking the oath, "I do solemnly swear that I will faithfully execute the office of the President of the United States and will, to the best of my ability, preserve, protect, and defend the Constitution of the United States," the president, his family, friends, and invited guests enjoyed the over $40,000,000 festivities of Inauguration Day.

ON MARCH 1, 2005, in the Roper v. Simmons case, the Supreme Court held that executing people who commit crimes before they turn eighteen constitutes cruel and unusual punishment, a violation of the Eighth Amendment. Writing the majority opinion, Justice Kennedy pointed out that since the United States is the only country in the world that officially allows the execution of juveniles, it should be considered unusual punishment.

ON AUGUST 25, 2005, Hurricane Katrina caused catastrophic damage on the Gulf coast, resulting in more than 1,000 deaths and leaving millions homeless.

AFTER HURRICANE KATRINA, FEMA's director, Michael Brown, testified that he informed White House officials on August 29 that the levees had breached and the city was flooding, but the Bush administration stated that they did not hear of the breach until August 30. Even when a Senate committee requested documents during an investigation of the government's response to the disaster, the White House refused, claiming confidentiality.

AFTER HAVING SERVED on the Supreme Court for thirty-three years, nineteen of those as chief justice and fourteen as an associate justice (Nixon appointee), Chief Justice William Rehnquist died on September 3, 2005. He was succeeded by John Roberts, who became the seventeenth chief justice of the U.S. Supreme Court.

THE WAR IN IRAQ continued through 2003 in spite of the orchestrated "Mission Accomplished" claim of President Bush on May 1, 2003. Following increased fighting, speculation about the administration's misuse of intelligence, and the realization that the war was going to last longer than originally hoped, good news came in December with the capture of Saddam Hussein. Trials for crimes against humanity and genocide began in October 2005. In November 2006, Hussein was sentenced to death by hanging; the execution took place on December 30, 2006.

ARTICLE I, SECTION 8, of the United States Constitution gives Congress the power to declare war. The last war in United States history that was declared by Congress was World War II. Since that time the United States has fought in the Korean War, Vietnam War, Persian Gulf War, Afghanistan War, and Iraq War, none of which were declared by the United States Congress.

BETWEEN JANUARY 4 AND JANUARY 9, 2006, hundreds died at the hands of suicide bombers. In April the European Parliament announced that the CIA had conducted more than 1,000 secret flights over Europe, apparently transporting terrorism suspects to countries that would allow torture.

THE MONTH OF JULY 2006 was the deadliest month of the Iraq war for Iraqi citizens with 3,438 civilian deaths. According to American military authorities, as reported in the *New York Times*, bomb strikes against American and Iraqi security forces numbered 1,666 in the month of July.

IN 2002, INTELLIGENCE REPORTS stated that Iran had built a large uranium plant without informing the United Nations. Satellite photographs confirmed that nuclear sites existed in Iran, and after the United States accused Iran of developing weapons of mass destruction, Iran agreed to inspections by the International Atomic Energy Authority. In 2005 Hardliner Mahmoud Ahmadinejad was installed as Iranian president, and Iran pledged an "irreversible" resumption of uranium enrichment. On January 3, 2006, Iran announced it would restart its nuclear energy program.

THE 2006 MIDTERM ELECTIONS were as heated and contentious as elections can be. While the Republicans were desperately trying to hold on to both chambers of Congress in order to continue to endorse the Bush administration's agenda, the Democrats had hopes of regaining both houses of Congress, something they had not done since 1994.

When the votes were counted, the Democrats had taken back both the House of Representatives with a gain of twenty-nine seats and the Senate with a gain of six seats.

IN MID-DECEMBER 2005, an article in the *New York Times* revealed that the Bush administration had been conducting wiretapping of United States citizens without court-issued warrants from the United States National Security Agency. This was confirmed by Attorney General Alberto Gonzales and was contrary to an earlier statement the president had made when he said that "the government did not wiretap without getting a court order."

ON AUGUST 17, 2006, a federal court ruled that the wiretapping was a violation of the Fourth Amendment but allowed the practice to continue pending an appeal by the federal government. In addition, Congress began working on a number of bills that would expand the president's power to conduct the surveillance with the authority of statute.

MILITARY COMMISSIONS USED to try suspects at Guantanamo Bay Prison had been the subject of debate for some time when the Supreme Court decided on June 29, 2006, that the commissions were a violation of both the Geneva Conventions and the separation of powers within the federal government. Following the ruling, the Bush administration had to seek authorization through statute from Congress. During September 2006, both the House of Representatives and the Senate passed the Military Commissions Act of 2006, allowing the president authority to use the military commissions.

THE USE OF THE MILITARY TRIBUNAL to bring enemy forces to trial has been employed in our history by General George Washington during the American Revolution, President Lincoln during the Civil War, and President Franklin D. Roosevelt during World War II.

ON MAY 25, 2006, a Houston jury found Kenneth Lay and Jeffrey Skilling, former chief executives of Enron, guilty of fraud and conspiracy. Lay was convicted of six counts of fraud and conspiracy and four counts of bank fraud.

Skilling was found guilty of eighteen counts of fraud and conspiracy and one count of insider trading. Kenneth Lay died of heart failure on July 5, 2006, at the age of sixty-four. Ironically, Lay's death would result in his conviction being vacated and would make it all but impossible for the government and investors to recover money from the Lay estate. Civil suits against his estate are still pending.

ON JUNE 7, 2006, the United States Senate defeated an amendment that would have banned same-sex marriage and on June 28 voted down an amendment that would have given Congress the power to stop flag desecration.

ALTHOUGH ATTEMPTS WERE made in 2006 to raise the minimum wage from $5.15 an hour to $7.25 an hour, the Republican majorities in the House of Representatives and Senate voted it down once again. At that time, the minimum wage had not been increased since 1997. It was finally increased to $7.25 an hour on July 24, 2009.

ON OCTOBER 9, 2006, North Korea tested a nuclear missile in defiance of the wishes of the world community. On October 14, the United Nations Security Council voted unanimously in favor of a resolution punishing North Korea for its reported testing of a nuclear weapon.

FOLLOWING POPULATION MILESTONES of 100 million in 1915 and 200 million in 1967, the United States reached 300 million on October 17, 2006.

INDEX